THE FEEL BETTER COOKBOOK

THE FEEL BETTER COOKBOOK

TASTY REMEDIES FOR COMMON AILMENTS

BY SUSAN A. SKOLNICK

WINGS BOOKS
NEW YORK • AVENEL, NEW JERSEY

Originally published under the title *The I Feel Awful Cookbook*
Copyright © 1985 by
National Press Books, Inc., and Susan A. Skolnick
All rights reserved.

This 1993 edition is published by Wings Books,
distributed by Outlet Book Company, Inc.,
a Random House Company
40 Engelhard Avenue, Avenel, New Jersey 07001,
by arrangement with National Press, Inc.

Random House
New York • Toronto • London • Sydney • Auckland

Printed and bound in the United States of America

Library of Congress Cataloging-in-Publication Data
Skolnick, Susan A., 1962-
[I feel awful cookbook]
The feel better cookbook : food remedies for
common ailments / by Susan A. Skolnick.
p.   cm.
Originally published: The I feel awful cookbook.
Bethesda, Md. : National Press, 1985.
Includes index.
ISBN 0-517-08910-6
1. Diet therapy.   2. Medicine, Popular.   I. Title.
RM216.S55   1993
615.8'54—dc20   92-38315
CIP

8 7 6 5 4 3 2 1

Acknowledgments

Many thanks to Norman Posel, Tim LaRonde and Grandma Bertha for their recipes. Thanks again to Norman for patiently tasting the oversweetened and undersalted as well as the just right.

To my parents.

Contents

Introduction

More than just a collection of recipes, *The Feel Better Cookbook* is a guide to eating when you're not feeling well. The concept of eating your way back to health involves several approaches: for some ailments, what you *avoid* eating is probably more important for healing than what you do eat; for others, general improvement of your diet results in overall health; and for some conditions, such as constipation, diet generally causes the problem, and diet can clear it up.

The history of foods as cures or causes of different illnesses is a rich mixture of fact and folklore. While some past beliefs have been disproved by modern science, such as chocolate as a cause of acne, and bland diets as a remedy for ulcers, others have been substantiated: a study at Mount Sinai Medical Center found that chicken soup can improve cold symptoms, and yogurt is often prescribed to help restore the beneficial bacteria in the digestive tract which have been destroyed by antibiotics. Along with dietary suggestions supported by conventional medicine, this book provides home or folk remedies which have worked for many people. Food and diet as therapy is still a controversial area, however, and these remedies are not replacements for medicine or medical care.

Food Allergies

About 15 percent of adults and 40 percent of children have some kind of food allergy, according to allergist Allan V. Giannini, M.D. Although many people can name a food which doesn't "agree" with them, often because it gives them indigestion, this reaction does not necessarily indicate a food allergy, in which specific food proteins cause the body to form antibodies and exhibit such varied symptoms as hives, wheezing, vomiting, cramps, diarrhea, headache, fatigue, irritability and depression.[1] Some physicians prefer to label "allergic" only those reactions which occur immediately, and often violently, after eating a certain food. Delayed, less obvious reactions to foods are then considered food *intolerances* or *sensitivities.*

The most common food allergens are milk products, eggs, wheat, corn, beans (which includes peanuts and licorice), seafoods, chocolate, cola, citrus fruits, tomatoes, cinnamon and artificial food colors.[2,3]Since the chances of developing a sensitivity to a particular food increases as more of the food is eaten, it is not uncommon for people to be sensitive to their favorite foods. On the other hand, an *aversion* to a certain food may indicate food allergy because the person once experienced a negative reaction after eating that food.

The most reliable way to diagnose a food allergy is to eliminate the suspected food from the diet for two to three weeks and see if symptoms disappear, and then return when the food is reintroduced.[4] If a person is uncertain about which foods may be causing a problem, a more strict elimination diet under the guidance of a doctor should indicate whether food allergy is present.

This book does not detail special diets for people with food allergies; for comprehensive discussions on this subject and recipes, see *Tracking Down Hidden Food Allergy,* by William G. Crook, M.D., and *The Best Guide to Allergy,* by Allan V. Giannini, M.D.

Basic Nutrition

Many of us react to the claims surrounding a new diet or vitamin supplement with a healthy dose of skepticism. There is so much nutrition quackery that many people suspect anything that is said, valid or not, about the harms or benefits of certain types of food. Nonetheless, "You are what you eat" is closer to the truth than many would like to realize; our diets can have a profound effect on our health. The U.S. Senate Select Committee on Nutrition stated in its report, *Dietary Goals for the United States,* that "most of all the health problems underlying the leading causes of death in the United States could be modified by improvements in diet . . . "

A recent study by the United States Department of Agriculture revealed that at least one-third of the American population consumed less than 70 percent of the Recommended Daily Allowance of calcium, iron, magnesium and vitamin B_6.[5] The nutrients that we do get can be depleted by stress, smoking, alcohol, pollution, food processing and preparation. Many of the symptoms dealt with in this book—headache, pre-menstrual syndrome, fatigue—can indicate marginal, or sub-clinical, deficiencies in certain nutrients. Rather than stepping into the sticky arena of vitamin and mineral supplements, this book concentrates on the foods which contain those nutrients.

Basics of a Healthful Diet

1. Make complex carbohydrates the foundation of your diet. That means less or no white bread, white rice, doughnuts, and Frosted Rice Krinkles, and more whole wheat bread, brown rice, beans, seeds, potatoes, bananas and other fresh fruits and vegetables. Rather than making meat the centerpiece of most dinners, use smaller amounts and think of it as a side dish or even as a condiment to add flavor to vegetable and grain dishes.

2. By following number one, you will also be increasing your intake of fiber, found in fresh fruits and vegetables, whole grains, beans, and seeds.

3. Cut down on or preferably eliminate refined sugar, alcohol and caffeine. The craving for these kinds of substances often decreases naturally as overall health improves. (*Note*—there is some evidence that a moderate amount of alcohol—about one glass of wine a day—may decrease the risk of heart attack. Regularly drinking much more than this, however, is definitely a health risk.)

4. Cut fat intake to about one-fifth of calories. Replace saturated fat—found in whole milk, butter, cream, fried foods, ice cream, and red meat—with polyunsaturated fat, found in beans, nuts and seeds.

5. For protein, emphasize lean meats, chicken, fish, beans and grains.

6. Decrease your intake of processed foods, fast foods, junk foods.

Notes

1. Giannini, Dr. Alan, *The Best Guide to Allergy*, Appleton-Century-Crofts, New York, 1981.

2. Ibid.
3. Galton, Lawrence, *1,001 Health Tips,* Simon and Schuster, New York, 1984.
4. Giannini, op. cit.
5. Pao, Eleanor, "Problem Nutrients in the United States," *Food Technology,* September, 1981.

PART 1
Viruses

Chapter One

Colds and Flu

Infections and fever increase the body's need for liquids, protein, B vitamins, vitamin A, vitamin C and other nutrients. One's appetite, however, usually wanes. Since most people have sufficient stores of nutrients in their bodies to last for several days, a lack of food generally does not slow one's recovery. As recovery begins and your appetite returns, make an extra effort to eat nourishing foods to replenish protein, calories, and nutrients. Fluid intake is vital during illness to prevent dehydration. Thirst should not be used as a gauge for fluid needs; you can lose a considerable amount of fluid before your brain sends out the thirst signal.[1]

Colds

With a stuffy head and congested nasal passages blocking your sense of taste, food loses its appeal. Inhaling the steam from liquids like hot tea with honey and chicken soup will help loosen mucus and flush out infecting organisms. Foods laced with spices such as cayenne, chili pepper, garlic, mustard, horseradish, and Tabasco sauce also help to clear your sinuses and lungs, and have a strong enough flavor to alert your dulled tastebuds.

1

Garlic, a faithful home remedy, acts as an expectorant, and helps loosen congestion.

Chicken Soup: The Oldest Remedy

Viruses prefer a relatively cool environment, and usually thrive in the nasal passages where inhalation tends to keep things cool. A fever is the body's way of making itself less habitable to invading viruses. Inhaling the steam from a hot bowl of chicken soup will help kill viruses.

Even conventional medicine has supported the chicken soup remedy. A doctor from the Mount Sinai Medical Center compared the effect of chicken soup and hot and cold water on nasal clearance. Cold water made things worse, hot water helped a bit, but chicken soup provided the most relief.[2]

The therapeutic value of chicken soup is greatly enhanced when it is lovingly prepared (from scratch) and served by a dear relative or friend.

Tim's Chicken Soup

Start with a 6-7 pound roaster, cook it for dinner, and save half the meat and all of the carcass and bones for soup. This is Tim's killing-two-meals-with-one-bird method. The secret to this soup is to add the chicken *last,* so the individual pieces of meat retain their flavor. Notice measurements for spices are not given: make this soup a personal work of art.

> half of the meat from a 6-7 pound roaster, and bones
> 4-6 bouillon cubes
> salt and pepper
> onion powder
> garlic powder
> 1 bay leaf
> thyme
> basil
> 2-3 onions, chopped
> 2 carrots, chopped
> 1-2 celery stalks, chopped
> ½-1 green pepper, chopped
> other optional vegetables: potatoes, corn, green beans.
> 2-3 cups egg noodles

Fill a large pot two-thirds full of water.
Add chicken carcass, bones and spices to boiling water and boil for 2 hours or more.
Add bouillon cubes.
Strain liquid from pot, remove carcass and bones, then return liquid to pot.
Add vegetables and simmer for 30 minutes.
Add egg noodles and cook for 5-8 minutes.

Reduce heat and add chicken meat. Taste and adjust seasonings, and add more water if necessary.
Simmer for a few more minutes to allow chicken flavor to mingle with the soup.
Makes 1 big pot of soup.

Recipes

Spicy Broccoli

Full of vitamins and zing.

1 bunch broccoli
½ cup tomato juice
¼ teaspoon Tabasco
1 clove garlic, pressed
½ teaspoon salt
2 tablespoons wine vinegar
1/4 cup oil

Slice broccoli into small trees and steam about 10 minutes.
Make sauce while broccoli is steaming: Heat oil and garlic in a small saucepan. Add the rest of the ingredients and simmer.
Pour sauce over broccoli and serve.
Serves 3 to 4.

Spiced Miso Broth

Miso is high in protein and easy to digest. This fermented soybean paste is available in health food stores and Oriental groceries.

1 cup water
½ teaspoon grated ginger
1 teaspoon Worcestershire sauce
¼ teaspoon dry mustard
1 clove garlic, pressed
3 tablespoons chopped fresh parsley
3 tablespoons chopped scallions
½ tablespoon oil
1 tablespoon miso

Sauté garlic in oil until lightly browned.
Add water, and then ginger, Worcestershire sauce, and mustard.
Bring to a boil, add scallions, let simmer for 2 to 3 minutes.
Remove from heat. Add parsley.
Take about 3 tablespoons of the soup broth and add to a small bowl with the miso. Mix thoroughly with a fork or small whisk. Stir miso mixture into soup.
Serves 1.

Norman's Ultimate Vegetarian Spaghetti Sauce

This one will bring tears of joy to your eyes, and clear skies to your nasal passages.

    1 small onion, chopped
    2 tablespoons fresh basil or dill, chopped
    2 tablespoons fresh parsley (optional)
    2 large garlic cloves, sliced thin
    1 red or green pepper, chopped
    2 tablespoons olive oil
    1 tablespoon vegetable oil
    4-6 ounces extra firm tofu, chopped into small
        cubes
    16 ounces tomato sauce or
        1 6-ounce can of paste and 1½ cups water
    2 tablespoons grated Parmesan and Romano
        cheese (optional)
Spices: (Note that measurements are not exact. Although spicing is crucial to this sauce, it will not suffer markedly if you don't have some of the less common spices, such as fenugreek seed, coriander, or black mustard seeds.)
        healthy sprinkling dried basil (1 to 2 teaspoons)
        shake of black pepper (more or less to taste)
        dash cumin (very important to use at least a little
            of this spice)
        ½ to ¾ teaspoon chili powder
        dash allspice
        pinch of oregano (just a pinch: this sauce is proud
            not to depend on this spice)
        ⅛ teaspoon fenugreek seed (optional)
        pinch of coriander
        light sprinkling of black mustard seed
        ¼ teaspoon ginger

½ teaspoon thyme
cayenne pepper to taste (at least ½ teaspoon)
½ teaspoon salt

Pour oil into saucepan and add vegetables, garlic, tofu and spices.
Heat slowly on low heat, stirring to distribute oil and spices.
When food begins to simmer and fry:

If you're using tomato *paste:* Add enough water just to cover vegetables and tofu, then add can of tomato paste and stir. Add more water to make sauce a bit thinner than you will finally want it. (It will thicken with cooking.) Add cheese if desired. Cover and let simmer for 15 minutes, stirring occasionally.

If you're using tomato *sauce:* Add sauce, cheese if desired, cover and let simmer over low heat for 15 minutes, stirring occasionally.
Especially good served over spinach noodles.

Fever

By raising your body temperature and speeding up your metabolism, fever increases your need for liquids, protein, calories and other nutrients. Feed a cold, starve a fever? Old adages aside, there's no need to force yourself to eat if you're not hungry, nor to "starve" your fever if you are, however, you must drink plenty of fluids to prevent the dehydration which can accompany fever, vomiting and diarrhea. Juices and sodas generally contain too much sugar and can cause diarrhea. Dilute both juices and sodas (which have been allowed to go flat) by about half with water. A squirt of lemon will improve the flavor. Orange and grapefruit juices may irritate your stomach. Broths, soups and gelatins are all good sources of fluid.

Banana Freeze

This one goes down easily, and is surprisingly delicious.

1 frozen banana or
  1 banana and 3 ice cubes
½ teaspoon vanilla

Whiz ingredients in a blender and serve.
Serves 1.

Fruit Gel

Basic recipe:

    1 envelope unflavored gelatin or
        1½ teaspoons granulated agar
    2 cups fruit juice

For gelatin: Sprinkle gelatin over ½ cup fruit juice in a saucepan. Stir constantly over low heat until gelatin dissolves, 3 to 5 minutes.
Remove from heat, stir in remaining cold juice. Pour into serving dishes.
For agar: Sprinkle agar over 2 cups of juice in a saucepan. Let stand for a few minutes before stirring. Stir, and simmer for 5 minutes.
Pour into individual serving dishes and refrigerate.
Serves 4.
Variations: Mix juices (apple and orange, grape and pineapple. Add fresh or canned fruit (except for fresh or frozen pineapple, which interferes with gelling) to mixture after removing from heat.

Frozen Apple Yogurt

Smooth and icy, good for a fussy appetite or a sore throat.

1 cup plain yogurt
1 cup unsweetened applesauce
¼ teaspoon cinnamon
1 to 2 tablespoons maple syrup or honey

Whiz yogurt, syrup and cinnamon in a blender. Stir in applesauce.
Pour into individual containers and freeze for 3 to 4 hours.
Let soften 10 minutes before serving.
Serves 4.

Egg Drop Soup

    2 cups chicken broth
    1 teaspoon soy sauce
    1 teaspoon lemon juice
    ½ teaspoon sesame oil
    1 egg, lightly beaten

Bring broth to a boil.
Add soy sauce, lemon juice, and sesame oil. Lower heat and simmer for 5 minutes.
Drizzle egg into soup in a steady stream. Wait a few moments for the egg to set before stirring.
Stir and serve.
Serves 2.
Variations: Add 1 clove pressed garlic, a dash of cayenne pepper, and/or ginger for extra flavor.

Lemon Squash

Light and delicate.

> 1 yellow squash, sliced thin
> 1 zucchini, sliced thin
> ½ lemon, unpeeled and sliced in thin rounds
> 2 teaspoons honey
> ¼ cup water
> ¼ teaspoon cinnamon

Stir honey and cinnamon into water in a saucepan.
Add squash and lemon and bring to a boil. Cover and
simmer about 10 minutes until squash is tender.
Serve with the liquid for extra fluid and vitamins.
Serves 4.

Additional Suggestions

- yogurt with banana and a dash of vanilla extract
- cottage cheese melted on baked potato
- steamed rice cooked with canned, unsweetened peaches
- cooked cereal with applesauce
- toast topped with cottage cheese, applesauce, or sliced banana

Notes

1. Shangold, Mona M., *The Complete Book of Sports Medicine for Women,* Simon & Schuster, New York, 1985.
2. *Medical World News,* July 10, 1978.

Chapter Two

Herpes

Herpes hibernates in the nerve cells and emerges when the body's defenses are down. Many herpes sufferers can link their outbreaks of the virus with times when they are under stress or are not taking as good care of themselves. A good diet is vital in order for the body to resist infection. (See the basics outlined in the Introduction.)

A cure for herpes is not yet known, but according to several doctors and many herpes patients, a special nutritional program has been quite successful in lessening the severity and frequency of herpes attacks.

First some basic facts about the herpes virus. Type 1 herpes causes painful sores around the mouth (commonly known as cold sores or fever blisters or canker sores). Kissing and sharing food can transmit this type of herpes. Type 2 herpes causes sores to form around the genitals, and is usually transmitted by sexual intimacy. In some cases, genital herpes is caused by type 1 herpes.[1] Since herpes thrives in a moist environment, damp towels or fingers may be enough to transfer the virus. That means it is possible to give yourself genital herpes if you have type 1 herpes.

An outbreak of herpes is usually followed by a dormancy period, which can last from months to years. A recurrence is often triggered by emotional or physical stress (illness, lack of sleep, poor diet, surgery). Stress reduction is therefore vital in the management of herpes.

Herpes and Diet

In 1952, scientists discovered that lysine, an amino acid, suppressed the growth of a herpes virus in mice.[2] Further research a few years later found that the amino acid arginine *encouraged* the growth of the herpes virus, and in fact that herpes *requires* arginine to grow at all.[3,4]

Your body makes its own arginine, but you also absorb it from your diet.[5,6] The diet for herpes control features foods high in lysine and low in arginine. While thousands of herpes sufferers have hailed lysine as the only remedy to give them sustained relief from herpes attacks,[7] there is still some dispute in the scientific community over the efficacy of this treatment. Dr. Gabe Mirkin has stated that lysine treatment for herpes is ridiculous and scientifically unfounded. *The Saturday Evening Post* has carefully followed the herpes-lysine issue since it published its article "Does L-Lysine Stop Herpes?" in 1982. Since that time, hundreds of their readers have testified to the success of lysine treatment.

Doctors who encourage their herpes patients to increase their intake of lysine usually suggest that they use l-lysine supplements, which are available in health food stores. The usual recommendation is to take three 500 mg tablets three times a day on an empty stomach. If you want to take supplements, it's probably best to see a physician who prescribes lysine treatment. Here, we will concentrate on foods high in lysine and low in arginine. According to the theory, it is very important, even if you are taking lysine supplements, to avoid foods rich in arginine.

Following is a list of foods rich in l-lysine and l-arginine.

High L-lysine Foods (Foods to Eat)

Portion	Food	mg Excess L-lysine
4 oz	fresh fish	+ 930
4 oz	shark	+ 880
4 oz	canned fish	+ 810
4 oz	chicken	+ 740
4 oz	beef	+ 720
8 fl oz	goat's milk	+ 520
8 fl oz	cow's milk	+ 420
4 oz	lamb	+ 420
4 oz	mung beans	+ 410
4 oz	pork	+ 380
1 oz	cheese	+ 280
4 oz	beans, cooked	+ 270
4 oz	butter beans	+ 240
4 oz	cottage cheese, dry	+ 220
4 oz	mung bean sprouts	+ 210
1 tablet	brewer's yeast	+ 190
4 oz	crustaceans (crab, etc.)	+ 170
4 oz	soybeans, cooked	+ 130
8 fl oz	milk, human	+ 100
3 oz	green beans	+ 30
3 oz	dates	+ 20
4 oz	spinach	+ 20
4 oz	asparagus	+ 20
1	peach	+ 20
4 oz	eggplant	+ 10

High L-arginine Foods (Foods to Avoid)

Portion	Food	mg L-lysine Deficiency
3 oz	hazelnuts	− 2250
3 oz	Brazil nuts	− 2110
3 oz	peanuts	− 2060
3 oz	walnuts	− 810
3 oz	almonds	− 710
3 oz	cocoa powder	− 650
2 tablespoons	peanut butter	− 510
3 oz	sesame seeds	− 450
3 oz	cashews	− 420
3 oz	carob powder	− 310
3 oz	coconut	− 290
3 oz	pistachio nuts	− 240
4 oz	buckwheat flour	− 230
4 oz	chickpeas	− 210
4 oz	brown rice	− 190
3 oz	pecans	− 180
4 oz	oatmeal, cooked	− 130
3 oz	sunflower seeds	− 120
4 oz	corn	− 80
2 slices	whole grain bread	− 80
2 oz	wheat bran	− 80
4 oz	millet	− 60
1	yam	− 60
1	banana	− 30
2 slices	rye bread	− 30
2 oz	cabbage	− 30
4 oz	lentils	− 20
3 oz	grapes	− 20
3 oz	raisins	− 20
1	cucumber	− 20
1	tangerine	− 10

Source: Stop Herpes Now, by Dr. Barbara North, Ph.D., M.D., Thorsons Publishers Ltd., Northamptonshire, England, 1985.

Some qualifications: although cheese, eggs, whole milk, and red meat are high in l-lysine, the fat they contain may interfere with absorption.[8] Trim the fat on meats, emphasize poultry and unfatty fish, use low-fat milk and cheese, and avoid frying foods.

A look at the foods to avoid may be disturbing at first, since it probably contains many foods that you eat regularly. It is most important to avoid the foods which are especially high in arginine—nuts, seeds and chocolate. There's no need to give up all whole grains, although specialists suggest that you use them sparingly during an attack.[9] Try to balance your meals so that if you do eat a high-arginine food, you make up for it with high lysine food. (For example, drink milk with your oatmeal; eat cheese with your crackers.)

Low-protein foods such as fruits and vegetables are considered 'neutral.' The herpes diet should include generous quantities of these foods. In addition, if you don't already eat them, now is the time to discover the versatility and good taste of beans, tofu (soy bean curd) and tempeh (a fermented soy bean product.)

Lysine-rich Recipes

Sample Breakfasts

Cottage cheese and fruit.
Vegetable omelet.

Amaranth: the grain for herpes sufferers. You may not have heard of this Aztec grain, but its high protein content makes it an "elite" grain. Unlike most grains, amaranth is rich in lysine. And it is quite versatile: the leaves can be used in salads, the seeds can be cooked as a breakfast cereal or side dish, or popped like popcorn. You can find amaranth in most health food stores.

Lunches

If your typical lunch is a peanut butter and jelly sandwich with a chocolate bar (with nuts) for dessert, you are creating a hefty lysine deficiency. Try yogurt, chef salads, and stir-fries with chicken and vegetables. If you like sandwiches, fill them with cheese and vegetables, or bean spreads. (See *Tofu Spread in Chapter Three.*)

Barbecued Beans

1½ cups cooked kidney beans
1 onion
1 green pepper, chopped
1 clove garlic, pressed
1 tablespoon oil
3 tablespoons tomato paste
1 tablespoon lemon juice or vinegar
½ teaspoon soy sauce
(Note: if you're in a hurry, substitute prepared catsup for the above three ingredients)
1 teaspoon molasses
1 teaspoon chili powder
dash cayenne pepper, allspice, and nutmeg
water to thin sauce
salt and pepper to taste

Sauté onion, garlic and green pepper in oil until soft. In a small bowl, mix tomato paste, lemon juice, soy sauce, molasses, chili powder, and spices. Thin with a little water, taste, and adjust seasonings.
Add sauce to onions and peppers. Add beans. Simmer in pan for 10 minutes at low heat.

Sample Dinners

Mung Bean Soup (see recipe in Fatigue Chapter).

Replace spaghetti with bean thread or spaghetti squash, serve with *Norman's Ultimate Spaghetti Sauce* in Colds and Flu Chapter.

See *Tofu Sloppy Joes* and *Joel's Chicken Limón* in Chapter Ten.

See *Tempeh Barbecue* in Chapter Three.

Make pancakes and crusts using shredded potato, zucchini, rutabagas or turnips. A basic recipe is to mix 2 to 3 cups of coarsely grated vegetable with 1 beaten egg, 2 tablespoons of milk or yogurt and a little salt. Cook as pancakes in a skillet, or spread onto a baking sheet and cover with pizza toppings.

Remarkable Multi-Bean Soup

This soup will even woo non-bean-lovers.

6 cups water
1 teaspoon salt
1 onion, sliced
¾ cup dry pinto beans
¾ cup dry kidney beans
1½ cups white beans
1 bay leaf
3 tablespoon cumin
healthy dash of cayenne
2 tablespoon chili powder
1 teaspoon ginger
1 teaspoon honey
1 8-ounce can tomato sauce
1 6-ounce can tomato paste
1 green pepper, chopped

Boil water in a large pot. Add onions, beans, spices, and honey to boiling water.
Bring to a simmer, cover, and let cook over low heat for 1½ hours.
Stir in tomato sauce and paste and add green pepper.
Taste and adjust seasonings.
Cover and cook for 30-45 minutes until soup starts to thicken. If you can feel beans colliding with the spoon when you stir, it's not ready. Cook until you can stir more smoothly.
Serves 6 (or 2 for three dinners—it gets even better with age.)

Mock Noodle Soup

This soup is made with miso, a soybean paste available in health food stores, and tofu (bean curd), available in most supermarkets.

    4 cups water
    1 medium onion, chopped
    2 cloves garlic, pressed
    ¼ teaspoon freshly grated ginger
    1 teaspoon sesame oil
    2 teaspoons vegetable oil
    ¼ teaspoon cayenne pepper
    4 ounces tofu
    ½ green pepper, chopped
    2 tablespoons freshly minced parsley
    4 tablespoons miso

Sauté onions and garlic in sesame and vegetable oil while bringing water to boil in a soup pot.
Slice the tofu into thin strips to resemble noodles.
When water boils, add onions, green pepper, ginger, cayenne and parsley.
Simmer for 5 minutes, then add tofu and cook another minute.
Remove from heat. In a small bowl, mix the miso with 4 or 5 tablespoons of the hot soup broth until smooth. Pour the miso into the soup and stir well.
Serves 4.

Notes

1. Reeves, W.C., et al., 'Risk of recurrence after first episodes of genital herpes'. *New England Journal of Medicine,* 1983; 309(16).

2. Pearson, H.E., et al., 'Effect of certain amino acids and related compounds on propagation of mouse encephalomyelitis virus'. *Proceedings of the Society for Experimental Biology and Medicine,* 1952, 70:409-11.
3. Tankersley, R., 'Amino acid requirements of herpes simplex virus in human cells.' *Journal of Bacteriology,* 1964, 87:609-13.
4. Griffith, R.S., et al., 'A multicentered study of lysine therapy in herpes simplex infection'. *Dermatologia,* 1978, 156:257-267.
5. Lerner, J., *A Review of Amino Acid Transport Processes in Animal Cells and Tissues.* University of Maine at Orono Press, Orono, Maine 1978.
6. Leathem, J.H., (ed.), *Protein Nutrition and Free Amino Acid Patterns.* Rutgers University Press, New Brunswick, N.J., 1968.
7. Anon. 'Help membership HSV Survey Research Project Results'. *The Helper* (American Social Health Assoc.), 1981, 3(2):1-5.
8. North, Barbara, Ph.d., M.D., *Stop Herpes Now,* Thorsons Publishers Ltd., Northamptonshire, England, 1985.
9. Ibid.

PART 2
Gastrointestinal Distress

Chapter Three

Indigestion

If we were all sparklingly conscious beings, with body, mind and world fully integrated, our bellies would rarely, if ever, ache. Our gastrointestinal problems begin when we choose to savor goodies which our mouths want more than our stomachs.

Indigestion is often caused by overeating, or eating too quickly. Drugstore shelves lined with products to tame a "sour stomach" suggest that most of us suffer from dietary indiscretion at times. If your indigestion is a result of overindulgence, time and sincere repentance are the surest healers. Avoid lying down; take a brisk walk, and wait at least three hours before going to bed, if possible. Sipping water may help. If you drink tea, brew it lightly to avoid irritation from the caffeine. For your next meal (not before you're truly hungry), eat a light meal of non-irritating food (see recipes).

What Causes Stomach Upset?

① Eating too much.

② Greasy, fatty foods. Fatty foods stay in the stomach longer than other foods. The carbon dioxide created during the digestion of a fatty meal can distend the stomach and small intestine, causing an uncomfortable bloated feeling. Avoid lobster, crab, nuts and fried food if you feel predisposed to indigestion. Avoid eating large quantities of meat at one sitting: big burgers and thick slabs of sirloin take a long time to digest.

③ Foods which may cause indigestion include:
caffeine-containing beverages
milk
radishes
cucumbers
turnips
onions
peppers
chili
garlic*
mustard
curry
horseradish
aspirin
tomato products
orange juice and other citrus products

    * In some cases, garlic *aids* digestion: it contains a substance called allicin which promotes the secretion of digestive enzymes.[1]

④ Chewable vitamin C tablets can irritate the stomach lining. If you must take these, eat them with a meal (and brush your teeth afterwards; chewable C's can corrode tooth enamel).

While black pepper irritates the stomach lining, cayenne pepper aids digestion. Chili peppers are also supposed to facilitate the digestion of starches, increase gastric secretions, and stimulate appetite. Pineapples contain an enzyme called bromelin which aids in the

Chewing on a sprig of parsley is an old remedy for indigestion. At the very least, it will sweeten your breath.

digestion of protein. Pineapples cooked with meat can make it more tender and digestible.[2]

A diet low in niacin, a member of the B complex, may result in insufficient hydrochloric acid production in the stomach, and then indigestion.[3] Niacin is found in lean meats, poultry, fish, peanuts, brewers yeast, wheat germ and desiccated liver. All the B vitamins are vital to the health of the gastrointestinal tract.

Annoyances as common as indigestion are bound to generate a myriad of home remedies. The following suggestions may not cure you, but your indigestion may open your mind to experiment.

- Chew a sprig of fresh parsley.
- Eat a small piece of raw potato.
- Eat a stick of celery.
- Try papaya enzyme or digestive enzyme tablets sold in health food stores.
- Some people swear that a tablespoon of olive oil eases their gas pains. Not advised after a heavy meal.

Gas

Swallowing air is the most common cause of gas. You may not think you swallow much air, but talking with food in your mouth, eating quickly and gulping a drink all promote air swallowing. Smoking, chewing gum, sucking mints and drinking alcohol make you swallow air by generating saliva, which is full of air bubbles.

Foods which can cause gas include:

beans
celery

broccoli
raisins
cauliflower
brussels sprouts
onions
carrots
cabbage

These foods are not *guaranteed* to cause you grief, so don't eliminate them from your diet without experimenting. All the foods listed above are highly nutritious (a diet high in the cruciferous vegetables—cauliflower, broccoli, cabbage, brussels sprouts—has been linked with lower cancer incidence); their benefits surely outweigh the inconvenience of a little gas. Fibrous vegetables, as well as brewer's yeast, and high fiber breads, cereals, and crackers are especially likely to produce gas if you add them suddenly to your diet. Increase your fiber and brewer's yeast intake gradually, allowing your digestive system time to adjust. In addition, yogurt, lemon juice, and cider vinegar may reduce gas produced by high-fiber foods. Yogurt increases the bacteria in the colon which digests fibrous vegetables, and lemon juice and cider vinegar help break down cellulose.[4] Fortunately, these ingredients are ideal for salad dressings (see recipe).

On the other hand, you won't deprive your body of much nutritional value if you avoid carbonated beverages, whipped cream, beer, soufflés, and milk shakes, which contain a lot of air and can cause bloating and gas. When drinking a frothy beverage, don't guzzle; sip slowly, allowing the air bubbles to break in your mouth before swallowing.

Another frequent cause of gas is the consumption of dairy products by those who are lactose intolerant. The lactose (milk sugar) passes undigested into the colon where bacteria ferment the sugar, causing gas.[5] Some lactose intolerant people are able to digest fermented milk products such as yogurt, kefir, and buttermilk, because the lactose has been broken down by the fermentation process.

What to Do?

● If you have gas, avoid lying down. Physical activity helps to stimulate peristalsis—the waves of contraction in the intestine that pass its contents along—and to break down gas bubbles.

● A heating pad may ease gas pains.

● Charcoal tablets may provide relief if taken shortly after a meal. Charcoal seems to work by partially absorbing gas or the intestinal bacteria that produce gas.[6]

● A tablespoon of apple cider vinegar mixed in a glass of water is an old folk remedy for gas. The vinegar is supposed to help break down the cellulose in vegetables which can cause gas.

● Anise, fennel, and caraway seeds are said to be carminatives, which aid in expelling gas. Try chewing a few of these seeds after a particularly gassy meal. The seeds may also be used in cooking or brewed in tea.

● In addition to the above-mentioned seeds, *The Bowel Book* by David Ehrlich also recommends something called Blahende Tea. (*Blahende* is German for "windiness.") To make it, mix one-third teaspoonful each of valerian root, chamomile, and fennel seed (whole or ground) in a cup of boiling water. Strain after five minutes, and add a bit of lemon and honey. Sip slowly.

To avoid gas, try the following recommendations provided by the Digestive Diseases Clearinghouse:

- eat slowly and chew thoroughly;
- make sure dentures fit properly;
- avoid gum and hard candy;
- eliminate carbonated beverages;
- eat fewer gas-producing foods;
- avoid milk if lactose intolerant;
- try an exercise like sit-ups if distention is a problem.

Heartburn

Heartburn occurs when the valve between the esophagus and the stomach relaxes inappropriately or is very weak. This allows the highly acidic contents of the stomach to back up into the esophagus.

Peppermint, spearmint, caffeine, alcohol, decaffeinated coffee, chocolate, citrus fruits and juices, fried and fatty foods, tomato products and smoking can all weaken the esophagus sphincter muscle. The customary after-dinner mint, chocolate, cigarette and coffee can actually be the worst ways to complete a meal in terms of gastric comfort, especially if the meal featured rich or acidic foods.

Some people notice that certain foods eaten together tend to cause more heartburn or indigestion than when eaten separately. There is no definitive list, but possible troublemakers include yogurt and citrus, yogurt and coffee, and coffee and citrus.

Digestible Fare

These recipes feature foods which are easy to digest, contain nutrients which are essential to the health of the digestive tract, and/or aid digestion in some way.

Millet dishes

Millet is a very digestible grain, rich in niacin and magnesium, and versatile enough for breakfast, lunch, and dinner, in place of rice. You can find millet in health food stores and some supermarkets.

Basic Millet

> 1 cup millet
> 3 cups vegetable broth or water

Bring water to boil. Stir in millet.
Bring to a second boil. Reduce heat to simmer and cover pot.
Cook for about 30 minutes.
Serves 3.

Spiced Peach Gelatin

Gelatin is easy to digest. Agar-agar is a type of seaweed which may be used as an alternative to gelatin, and is also assimilated easily. Cinnamon is said to have a mild carminative effect on the stomach lining.

> 1/2 cup water
> 1/2 cup apple juice
> 1 teaspoon agar-agar, or 1 package unflavored gelatin
> 3/4 cup canned peaches packed in their own juice, chopped
> 1/2 teaspoon cinnamon

Bring water and juice to a boil.
Add agar-agar or gelatin. Reduce to simmer.
Add peaches and cinnamon. Simmer for five minutes.
Pour into four small glasses and refrigerate until gelled.

Serves 4.

Vegetable Miso Soup

Miso is a fermented soybean paste, easy to digest, and rich in protein and vitamin B_{12}. It is available in health food stores and Oriental groceries. Miso should not be boiled; to preserve its nutrients, add to soups right before serving.

Tofu (bean curd) is low in fat and also easy to digest. Tofu is available in most supermarkets, and, happily, does not retain the gas-producing properties of regular beans.

This soup makes a satisfying main dish, especially if you add a grain such as rice, bulgur or millet.

   1 quart water
   8 ounces tofu, cut into small squares
   2 tablespoons tamari or soy sauce
   4 large mushrooms, sliced thin
   1 cup snow peas, fresh or frozen
   1 egg, lightly beaten
   1 tablespoon grated fresh ginger root
   1 tablespoon miso paste

In a large pot, bring the water, ginger and tamari to a boil.
Add snow peas, mushrooms, and tofu.
Whisk miso and egg with a little bit of water in a separate bowl.
Simmer soup for about 20 minutes. Right before serving, remove pot from heat and stir in egg/miso mixture.

Tofu Spread

Sandwiches made with peanut butter or luncheon meats can cause indigestion. This spread is high in protein and low in fat.

      1 ounce tofu
      1/4 one avocado
      1 teaspoon tamari
      1 teaspoon wine vinegar
      1/2 teaspoon lemon juice

Mash tofu and avocado in a bowl.
Add the rest of the ingredients. Spread on whole grain bread.
Enough for 1 sandwich.

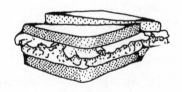

Tempeh

Tempeh, a cultured soybean product, is an ideal food, especially for anyone with a sensitive stomach. Tempeh is actually a "predigested" food: the fermentation process breaks down proteins, fats, the complex indigestible sugars in soybeans which cause gas; and phytates, substances in beans and grains which prevent minerals from being absorbed by the body.[7,8] Unlike tofu, which is bland until seasoned, tempeh has a unique flavor, and adapts especially well to dishes which usually require meat: tempeh burgers, sausages, egg rolls and casseroles are all delicious. Just steam tempeh 20 minutes and then use as ground beef.

Besides containing complete protein, tempeh offers a good supply of vitamin B_6, niacin, riboflavin, and vitamin B_{12}, a nutrient found mainly in animal products and which vegetarians must be sure to include in their diets. Tempeh is available in health food stores.

Tempeh Barbecue

> 8 ounces tempeh, steamed 20 minutes
> ⅓ cup honey
> ⅓ cup soy sauce
> ⅓ cup rice vinegar
> 1 teaspoon fresh ginger root, grated
> ½ teaspoon dry mustard

Cut tempeh into strips and place in a glass baking dish. Mix the honey, soy sauce, vinegar and ginger in a bowl and pour over tempeh. Cover and refrigerate for 2 hours. Preheat oven to 400° F. Pour excess marinade into a separate bowl.
Bake tempeh for 10-12 minutes, until dark brown.
Serve with rice.
Serves 4.

Parsley Dressing

This light and zesty dressing contains garlic, lemon juice, and, in a variation, yogurt—ingredients which can aid in digestion of fibrous vegetables. Garlic can be omitted if it causes indigestion.

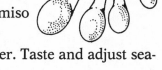

¼ cup oil
¼ cup water
2 tablespoons vinegar
½ tablespoon lemon juice
1 clove garlic
1 teaspoon soy sauce or miso
½ cup fresh parsley

Combine ingredients in a blender. Taste and adjust seasonings.

Makes a little over half a cup.

Variation: Add ¼ cup of plain yogurt.

Notes

1. Ehrlich, David, *The Bowel Book,* Schocken Books, New York, 1981.
2. Ibid.
3. Kirschmann, John D., Nutrition Almanac, McGraw-Hill, 1979.
4. Ehrlich, op cit.
5. Digestive Diseases Clearinghouse.
6. *Understanding Vitamins and Minerals,* Rodale Press, Emmaus, Pa., 1984.
7. Wagenknecht, A. C., et al, "Changes in Soybean Lipids During Tempeh Fermentation." *Journal of Food Science,* 26:373, 1961.
8. Shallenberger, R. S., et al, "Changes in Sucrose, Raffinose, and Stachyose During Tempeh Fermentation," *N.Y. State Agric. Exper. Stat.,* Geneva, N.Y.

Chapter Four

Diarrhea

The cause of this indelicate ailment may be obvious: you drank the water while touring Kathmandu and your intestinal tract took offense at the foreign bacteria. Diarrhea may also indicate the flu, inability to digest lactose (milk sugar), wheat-gluten sensitivity, or a reaction to other foods (anything from unripe fruit to eggs). Caffeine can stimulate colon activity, so coffee, cola or chocolate may be the aggravating factor.†

Some medicines, particularly antibiotics; high doses of vitamin C (over 3,000 milligrams a day), and the artificial sweeteners xylitol and sorbitol (found commonly in sugarless gum) may bring on diarrhea.[1] In the case of food or drug reactions, diarrhea usually subsides once the guilty item has been digested or eliminated.

Emotional stress can cause anything from a mild, temporary episode of diarrhea to a nasty chronic case. Diarrhea is a symptom of irritable bowel syndrome, a common gastrointestinal disorder which is often frustratingly unresponsive to treatment with drugs and special diets. Learning to handle stress is the best way to reduce symptoms of this disorder. Start by preparing your meals calmly and eating in a relaxed, unhurried manner.

---

† Black tea also contains caffeine, but generally does not cause diarrhea: the tannin in tea actually has a constipating effect.

What to Eat

If you have diarrhea, avoid foods containing fat or oil—salad dressings, sauces, and anything buttered, fried or sauteed. Prunes, onions, grapes, rhubarb, citrus fruits, and milk can all aggravate diarrhea. Sugar draws fluid into the digestive tract, so sweets should not be eaten, and fruit juices and soft drinks should be diluted with water. Avoidance of dairy products is often recommended for diarrhea, although yogurt may be beneficial, especially in the treatment of severe diarrhea in children.[2] Yogurt apparently helps to restore a healthy bacterial environment in the colon.

The BRATT Diet

A traditional remedy for diarrhea, the BRATT diet includes Bananas, Rice, Applesauce, Toast, and weak Tea. These foods are generally nonirritating, and may be good choices if you are suffering from acute, temporary diarrhea caused by intestinal flu or food poisoning. Apples and bananas contain pectin, the substance which causes fruit jellies to set, and is used in anti-diarrhea drugs.[3]

The BRATT diet is not nutritionally balanced enough to follow for any long period of time. In the case of chronic diarrhea, the traditional low-fiber, bland diet may actually do more harm than good; recent evidence indicates that dietary fiber *normalizes* bowel activity, making it effective for both constipation and diarrhea.[4]

Since the body can lose vital fluids and minerals during an attack of diarrhea, it is important to replace lost fluids and nutrients by drinking broth, weak tea or herbal tea, and juices diluted with water or herb tea.

Home Remedies

Cinnamon

As a folk medicine, cinnamon is used to ease nausea and alleviate diarrhea.[5] A cinnamon stick in a cup of herb tea is especially appealing to children. Cinnamon can also be sprinkled over applesauce or bananas.

Apples

Grated apples allowed to brown is a another home remedy for diarrhea. Apples have a laxative effect on some people, so you will have to experiment. Simmer apple gratings with a little water in a saucepan over low heat.

Carrots

Strained carrots and carrot soup for diarrhea enjoyed the endorsement of the medical community about 30 years ago.[6] Carrots, like apples, contain pectin, which can ease diarrhea. Many recipes for carrot soup contain milk or cream, which can aggravate diarrhea, even if you are not sensitive to dairy products when you are healthy. Try the following recipe without dairy products.

Carrot Soup

3 cups vegetable or chicken broth
3 carrots, diced
1 stalk celery
¼ cup chopped fresh parsley
1 tablespoon oil
1 cup chopped spinach, kale or other greens

Combine carrots, celery, parsley and oil in a soup pot. Cover and warm for 5 minutes.

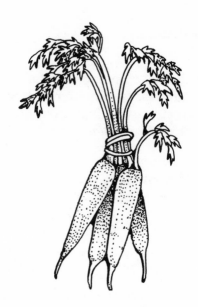

Add broth, salt if necessary. Cover and simmer for 30 minutes.
Add greens and cook for 5 minutes longer.
Serves 2 to 3.

Potatoes

Baked potatoes are usually a soothing choice, but replace the sour cream and butter with cottage cheese.

Cottage Cheese Topping

½ cup cottage cheese
1 tablespoon wheat germ
1 tablespoon chopped fresh parsley
1 teaspoon chopped fresh basil

Mix ingredients in a small saucepan.
Heat to a simmer, serve over split baked potatoes.

Bananas

Choose only very ripe bananas—unripe ones may make diarrhea worse. Eat them:

- plain
- frozen: peel bananas, wrap in plastic wrap, freeze. Eat whole, sliced, or blend in blender or food processor.
- cooked with rice or oatmeal.

Blueberries

Both blueberries and blackberries contain tannins, which reduce the amount of fluid that enters the digestive tract and tightens intestinal muscles. These berries have brought relief to many sufferers of chronic diarrhea.

Blueberry Spread

1 cup blueberries
2 tablespoons honey (more or less to taste)
3 teaspoons lemon juice

Combine ingredients in a saucepan and bring to a boil. Simmer for 3 minutes. Chill if desired.

Spread on whole grain toast, or stir into plain yogurt. *Makes 1 cup.*

Notes

1. Bricklin, Mark, *Rodale's Encyclopedia of Natural Home Remedies*, Rodale Press, Emmaus, PA 1982
2. Ibid, p.444
3. Allen, O.E., *The Secrets of a Good Digestion*, p. 43, Time-Life Books, Chicago, 1982
4. Smith, Lendon, M.D., *Feed Yourself Right*, McGraw Hill, 1983
5. Buchman, Dian D., *Herbal Medicine*, David McKay, 1979, p. 46
6. Bricklin, Mark, Op. Cit.

Chapter Five

Constipation

A caveman with constipation was undoubtedly a rarity. Constipation is a misery of modern civilization. Lack of exercise, overconsumption of refined foods, repeatedly ignoring the "call of nature," dieting, emotional stress and modern toilet seats can all contribute to a sluggish bowel.

Diet

Meat, white bread so soft you can roll it into a little ball, and canned fruits and vegetables skinned and boiled to mush all lack the roughage necessary to maintain regularity. Foods with roughage—fresh fruits and vegetables, whole grains, beans, seeds—absorb moisture to soften the stool and provide the bulk necessary to trigger the bowels to move. Foods which contain tannins—tea, blueberries, blackberries—can cause constipation because tannins reduce the amount of fluid that enters the digestive tract and tighten intestinal muscles.

Regular constipation due to a low-fiber diet has been linked to more serious health problems. Women with severe constipation due to low fiber diets have a higher incidence of precancerous lesions of the breast.[1] Some

A spoonful of corn or wheat bran, *ac-companied by a glass of water,* is a tried and true remedy for constipation.

researchers have also postulated that the fiber which relieves constipation also helps dilute and flush carcinogens from the intestinal tract.

Bran

Some people find relief if they add a spoonful of bran to their cereal or stir it into juice. Just sprinkling bran on food, however, is not enough; you must be sure to get plenty of liquid along with it—bran does its work by absorbing fluid and exerting pressure on the colon. Do not expect *immediate* relief from bran: it takes 24 hours for your body to process bran. Corn bran contains more fiber than wheat bran, and is supposed to relieve constipation more effectively. The fiber in oat bran has been found to reduce blood levels of LDL cholesterol (the "bad cholesterol"), but is a less effective bowel stimulant than wheat or corn bran.[2]

Other Fibers

Cellulose and hemicellulose are the types of fiber which best relieve constipation.[3] These fibers are found in the following foods:

Apples
Lima Beans
Bananas
Peaches
Beets
Peanuts
Bran and whole-grains
Pears
cereals
Brazil nuts

Rhubarb
Brussels sprouts
Strawberries
Cabbage
Tomatoes
Carrots
Whole wheat flour

Some Sticky Seeds

Two very effective constipation-relievers are flax seed and psyllium seed. These seeds contain mucilage, a sticky substance that helps lubricate the passage of food through the intestine. Soak seeds in water overnight and then add to hot cereals, stir-fry dishes, breads or muffins, or eat a spoonful plain. Start with a teaspoon of seeds and work up to a tablespoon per day. These seeds can often do their work within 24 hours.

Other Laxative Foods[4]

• *Garlic* is supposed to have a stimulating effect on the walls of the stomach and intestine.

• *Agar-agar* is a seaweed used as a jelling substance which helps regulate the bowels by forming slippery bulk in the intestinal tract. Agar may be used as a substitute for gelatin or as a base in soups and puddings. Other varieties of seaweed (dulse, wakame, kombu, hiziki) also provide excellent bulk for the intestines. These are usually sold dry and can be added to soups and casseroles.

• *Yogurt* contains lactic acid which acts as a gentle stimulant to the digestive tract.

• *Sauerkraut, sour pickles, and sour rye bread,* like yogurt, promote the growth of healthy bacteria in the intestines which help maintain regularity.

Dieters

Dieters may suffer from constipation for several reasons. One is that they are eating small amounts of foods, often low fiber foods such as cottage cheese and yogurt, and so have little residue to pass. Dieters may also over-restrict their intake of fats and oils, depriving their intestines of necessary lubrication. Dieters are wise to skip french fries and buttered bread, but it is important for overall health to eat some foods which provide natural fats, such as beans, seeds, nuts, fish, eggs, grains and meat.

Constipation in Children

An allergy to cow's milk may be the cause of constipation, especially in children. The simplest way to check for a milk sensitivity is to see if symptoms disappear after eliminating milk and milk products from the diet (yogurt, cheese, butter, anything containing whey or caseinate), and then reappear within 48 hours after a "milk challenge." Reactions occurring with three challenges is generally considered an indication of milk sensitivity.[5]

See recipes for milk substitutes in the Chapter 10.

Recipes

Liquid Breakfast

A tall beverage drunk first thing in the morning is an effective way to stimulate peristalsis (the waves of contraction passing along the intestine and forcing its contents onward). A spoonful of bran adds extra fiber.

½ cup fruit juice
½ cup water
½ banana
1 teaspoon vanilla
1 egg yolk
1 tablespoon bran (less if you are new to bran)
2-3 ice cubes

Blend all ingredients in a blender.

Apple-Raisin Medley

Serve for dessert or breakfast; prunes, figs, or dates can be substituted for or mixed with raisins.

2 large apples, shredded
1 tablespoon butter or margarine
¼ cup chopped walnuts or pecans
¼ cup raisins
¼ teaspoon cinnamon
½ teaspoon lemon juice
2 tablespoons honey (optional, depending on your sweet tooth)

Sauté shredded apple in butter for one to two minutes. Add nuts, raisins, cinnamon, lemon juice and honey. Cook over low heat, stirring occasionally, for about five minutes.
Serves 2.

Bulgur Breakfast Cereal

⅓ cup bulgur
½ cup water
½ cup apple or grape juice
1 teaspoon soaked flax or psyllium seeds (soak
   overnight
chopped walnuts
half a banana, sliced

Bring water and apple juice to a boil. Add bulgur.
Lower heat and simmer for 20 minutes.
Stir in flax seeds, sliced banana and chopped nuts.
Serves 1.

Two Types of Tsimmes

Tsimmes is a traditional Jewish dish which often contains prunes, sweet potatoes, and/or carrots, but is actually any combination of meat and/or vegetables and/or fruits.

Grandma Bertha's Tsimmes

½ pound prunes, chopped
5 sweet potatoes, cut in chunks
1 tablespoon butter or margarine
¼ teaspoon salt
3 tablespoons lemon juice
2 tablespoon honey

Melt butter in a large pot.
Add salt, lemon juice and honey.
Stir in prunes and sweet potatoes.
Cover with four cups cold water and cook slowly for about one hour, until there is about ½ cup of juice left.
Serves 8.

Tsimmes #2

4 sweet potatoes, cut in chunks
3 carrots, sliced
1 cup pineapple juice
nutmeg
cinnamon
butter or margarine

Steam carrots and potatoes for about 20 minutes.
Put in baking dish. Add a pinch of nutmeg to pineapple juice and pour over vegetables.
Sprinkle cinnamon over top and dot with butter.
Bake at 350 ° F for 1 hour.
Serves 6.

Spiced Applesauce

3 cooking apples, chopped in small pieces (do not
  peel skins)
¼ cup water
½ tablespoon lemon juice
⅛ teaspoon each of cinnamon, cloves, mace and
  nutmeg
dried fruit: depending on what you have; sample
  combinations: 1 prune, 2 dates, 1 fig, chopped;
  or 1 tablespoon of raisins

Mix water, lemon juice and seasonings together in a
saucepan.
Add apples and dried fruit and bring to a boil.
Lower heat and simmer, covered, for 15 minutes.
Mash with a heavy fork or blend in blender for a
smoother sauce.
Serves 4.

Best Bran Muffins

  2 tablespoons oil
  ¼ cup or less molasses
  1 egg
  3/4 cup milk
      or 3/4 cup water mixed with 2 teaspoons
      soy powder
  1 cup bran
  1 cup whole wheat flour
  2 teaspoons baking powder
  ⅛ teaspoon baking soda
  ½ teaspoon salt (optional)
  ¼ cup raisins, chopped prunes, chopped figs (sim-
      mered in boiling water for 10 minutes)

Before starting, pour boiling water over dried fruit and
let soak.

Whisk egg with a fork in a bowl, add milk, molasses and oil.

Add bran, stir, and set aside.

In another bowl, mix dry ingredients and softened dried fruit, then add liquid ingredients. Mix gently (do not overbeat).

Fill muffin tins two-thirds full and bake about 20 minutes at 375 °F.

Notes

1. Petrakis, N.L., and King, F.B., "Cytological abnormalities nipple aspirates of breast fluid in women with severe constipation.," *Lancet* ii:1203-1205, 1981.
2. Kritchevsky, David, *Dietary Fiber in Health and Disease,* Plenum Press, 1982.
3. *Prevention,* September, 1984.
4. Ehrlich, David, *The Bowel Book,* Schocken Books, New York, 1981.
5. *British Medical Journal,* Vol. 287, November 26, 1983, p. 1593.

Chapter Six

Ulcers

The hydrochloric acid in your stomach is strong enough to dissolve iron. Normally, mucous secretions keep the stomach from digesting itself. An ulcer develops when there is an imbalance between the powerful digestive juices and the protective secretions.

A duodenal ulcer, the most common type of ulcer, is a sore in the small intestine, and is often characterized by a gnawing or hunger type of pain several hours after a meal. The pain is usually located in the upper abdomen, under the rib cage, and may wake you up during the night. Eating may relieve the pain temporarily.

A less common gastric ulcer is a sore in the stomach which may cause continuous pain or no pain at all. Eating may or may not bring relief.

Emotional stress, smoking and aspirin can cause ulcers, and aggravate existing ones. Smoking tends to reduce the body's production of bicarbonate, which helps neutralize stomach acid, and makes an ulcer more likely to bleed.[1] Aspirin can inflame the stomach lining. The caffeine in coffee, tea, and cola drinks can also be irritating.

What to Eat?

No diet exists that's been scientifically proven to cure ulcers, including the old, commonly prescribed "bland diet." Milk, until recently the classic ulcer remedy, can make matters worse because the calcium and protein actually stimulate gastric acids. If you have an ulcer, avoid milk and cream between meals, and consume very little of them at meals. You'll also want to avoid coffee (regular and decaffeinated), tea, cola, and alcohol, all of which strongly stimulate acid production.

Although no specific ulcer diet exists, individual ulcer sufferers know there are certain foods which seem to either aggravate or ease their gastric distress. Spicy or acidic foods may or may not irritate your ulcer. You'll have to experiment with different foods and see. While some doctors recommend switching from three meals a day to six smaller ones, others note that because eating generates stomach acid, it's best to stick with the three meals a day. Again, you'll have to see for yourself. If you are awakened by burning pains in the early morning, see if omitting your late-night snack makes a difference.

In order to optimize the body's ability to heal itself, ulcer sufferers will want to pay close attention to their diets' nutritional value. The problem with a bland diet is that it lacks the fiber and B vitamins necessary to keep the gastrointestinal tract functioning smoothly. Whole wheat bread, brown rice, and whole grain cereals contain the fiber and B vitamins essential in the maintenance of muscle tone in the GI tract.

Vitamins A, C, and E are all vital to help stimulate mucous production, reduce scarring and promote healing.[2] Good sources of these nutrients include fish liver oil (vitamin A), carrots, green leafy vegetables, broccoli, green peppers, fresh fruit, whole raw seeds and nuts, and wheat germ.

Home Remedies

Natural remedies available at health food stores include okra powder, slippery elm powder and kudzo powder. These plant-derived substances coat the digestive tract before it begins producing acid. Mix a spoonful of one of the powders with a little warm water and drink before eating.

Two other home remedies worth trying: plantain bananas and cabbage juice. Cabbage juice—mixed with carrot juice, celery juice, or tomato juice to improve the flavor—is supposed to work wonders. Unfortunately, juicing cabbages and carrots requires a juicer, not an inexpensive appliance. Plantain bananas may help prevent and heal ulcers, according to British researchers who studied the effect of powdered plantain on ulcers in small animals. [3] Plantain bananas must be cooked before eating. They may be boiled and then seasoned, or sliced thin and pan-fried in a small amount of oil.

Recipes

The recipes in this chapter contain nutrients important to healing and the health of the digestive tract.

A-B-C-E Loaf

This wholesome concoction provides vitamin A in the carrots, B vitamins in the brown rice and nutritional yeast, vitamin C in the peppers, and vitamin E in the eggs.

 3 carrots
 1 onion
 1 green pepper
 1/2 cup sunflower seeds
 1/2 cup walnuts
 2 eggs
 1 cup cooked brown rice
 2 tablespoons nutritional yeast (optional)
 2 teaspoons tamari
 1/4 teaspoon each, basil and thyme

Grate carrots and onion. Chop pepper.
Grind seeds and nuts in a blender.
Beat eggs lightly in a bowl.
Add tamari, spices and yeast to eggs. Mix all ingredients together in a large bowl, then pour into an oiled 9x5 baking dish.
Bake at 350 °F. for 30 minutes.
Serves 6 to 8.

Bulgur with Broccoli

This dish is simple but always pleasing. Vitamin A and C in the broccoli; B vitamins and fiber in the bulgur (cracked wheat) and almonds.

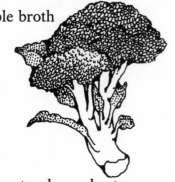

1 cup bulgur
2 cups water or vegetable broth
1 onion, chopped
1 bunch broccoli
1½ tablespoons oil
¼ cup slivered almonds
1 clove garlic, pressed
½ teaspoon ginger
1 tablespoon soy sauce
1 tablespoon honey

Add cracked wheat to boiling water, lower heat, cover, and let simmer for 20 minutes.
Sauté onion and garlic in oil until soft.
Chop broccoli into flowerets. Scrape the stalks with a vegetable peeler to reveal the softer, sweeter inside and slice into thin rounds.
Add broccoli to onions in pan, lower heat and cover for 5 minutes.
In a small dish, mix soy sauce, honey and ginger.
When cracked wheat is cooked, add to vegetables. Add soy sauce mixture and almonds and stir to mix well.
Cook for another 5 minutes.
Serves 4.

More recipes with nutrients important for healing ulcers:

Carrot Soup in Chapter 4.
Bran Muffins in Chapter 5.

Millet in Chapter 3.
Tsimmes in Chapter 5.

Notes

1. Alexander, Jan, "Ulcers—No More Bland Food," *Ms.*, October 1984.
2. Rohé, Fred, *The Complete Book of Natural Foods*, Shambala, Boston, 1983.
3. *British Journal of Pharmacology*, vol. 82, 1984

PART 3
Aches, Pains, and Lassitude

Chapter Seven

Headaches

Headaches may visit us for a vast number of reasons:

o   emotional stress, which often causes us to tense the jaw and neck
o   inhaling noxious fumes
o   exposure to too much sun
o   artificial sweeteners in diet drinks and sugarless gums
o   sleeping with your head under the covers, which can deprive you of oxygen
o   grinding your teeth at night
o   sitting in a smoke-filled room
o   ceasing to drink coffee suddenly if you have a regular habit. (Don't just keep drinking it, however. Cut down gradually.)
o   too much alcohol
o   a trauma to the head.

Since headaches can be symptoms of more serious problems, anyone plagued by chronic headaches should see a doctor.

Eating Habits

What you eat (and when and how) can also affect the status of your head. Some foods contain substances which cause the blood vessels in the head to dilate (resulting in a migraine or vascular headache). Low blood sugar due to missing a meal or fasting can cause headaches. Headaches may also signal an allergic reaction to a certain food. Foods more likely to be allergens which cause migraines include:[1]

wheat	sugar
citrus fruits	legumes
grapes	yeast
chocolate	pineapple
milk	coconut
nuts	tea
beef	coffee
pork	cola drinks
corn	

To determine if you have a sensitivity to any of these foods, see the Food Allergy section in the Introduction.

Many migraine sufferers are sensitive to vasoactive foods, which dilate the blood vessels in the head. A list of such foods to avoid follows. Try omitting them from your diet entirely for one week, and then reintroduce one food at a time and note the reaction. Since you may react immediately or several hours after ingesting the food, wait at least 24 hours before reintroducing another food.

Foods Which May Cause Migraines[3]

o Ripened cheeses: Cheddar, Emmentaler, Gruyere, Stilton, Brie and Camembert
o Herring
o Chocolate
o Vinegar (white vinegar permitted)
o Anything pickled, fermented or marinated

o   Sour cream, yogurt
o   Nuts, peanut butter, sunflower seeds, pumpkin seeds, sesame seeds
o   Hot fresh breads, coffee cakes, doughnuts, etc.
o   Any foods containing monosodium glutamate (MSG); often in canned soups and Oriental food
o   Onions
o   Canned figs
o   Citrus fruits (no more than one serving a day: one orange, one grapefruit, one glass orange juice)
o   Bananas (no more than one-half banana per day)
o   Raisins
o   Papayas
o   Excessive tea, coffee, and cola beverages (no more than two cups total per day)
o   Avocado
o   Fermented sausage (processed meats such as ham, hot dogs, bologna, salami, pepperoni, and summer sausage)
o   Chicken livers
o   All alcoholic beverages. If you must drink, limit yourself to no more than two normal-size drinks of Scotch, Vodka, Riesling, or Haute Sauterne.

Nutrition

Headaches may indicate a deficiency of B vitamins, which may develop if your diet is high in refined carbohydrates such as white bread, sugar, and white rice. Regular consumption of these processed foods, and especially of sugar, is so widespread that subclinical B vitamin deficiencies are not uncommon.[2] Smoking, alcohol, sleeping pills, estrogen (oral contraceptives), and sulfa drugs can also deplete the body's supply of B vitamins. Good B vitamin sources include wheat germ, brewer's yeast, liver, lean meats, and whole grains.

Eating Suggestions for Headache Victims

Make sure you drink enough fluids: dehydration can cause headaches. Water, seltzer water and herb teas contain no calories, sugar or caffeine, so you can drink them frequently throughout the day. Soda, coffee, and regular tea contain too much sugar and caffeine. It's also probably wise to limit the amount of fruit juice you drink, especially on an empty stomach, since the fructose (fruit sugar) breaks down quickly, and can play as much havoc with your blood sugar level as the sugar in cherry pop.

Natural Soda

> ½ cup seltzer water or club soda
> ½ cup fruit juice
> 1 teaspoon lemon juice
> ice

Mix in a glass.

Breakfast

Most people, though they may be willing to experiment at other meals, know what they like (or can stomach) for breakfast. The recipes below improve upon common types of breakfasts by providing more vitamins and fiber, and cutting down on sugar and fat.

If you have no appetite in the morning, and start the day with a cup of coffee and then a doughnut at mid-morning, you may find your head throbbing by noon. Instead, try a hot beverage without caffeine and take a high-protein, complex carbohydrate snack with you, such as whole grain crackers or muffins with nut butter or cheese, a piece of fruit and some nuts, or plain yogurt mixed with fruit and wheat germ, and eat it when you do get hungry.

A New Look at Toast

Instead of white bread with butter and jam, try whole grain toast spread with peanut, almond, cashew, or sunflower butter, and topped with sliced apple, pear, banana, raisins or dates.

Sesame Squares

These can be eaten as snacks as well as breakfast. Add another ½ cup of honey for a delicious dessert. Note that this recipe contains nuts and seeds, which cause migraines in some people.

> 2 eggs
> 2 tablespoons honey
> 1 tablespoon molasses
> ⅜ cup whole wheat flour
> ¼ teaspoon salt

1 cup chopped nuts (a mixture of walnuts, sun-
    flower seeds, cashews and almonds is ideal)
½ cup sesame seeds (hulled)

Preheat oven to 350° F. and oil a 9 inch square baking
pan.
Beat eggs lightly; mix in honey.
Stir in the rest of the ingredients and pour into pan.
Bake for 20 to 25 minutes.
Cool and cut into squares while still in pan.
Makes 12-15 squares.

High Pro Pancakes

   3 eggs
   ⅓ cup cottage cheese
   ¼ cup wheat germ
   2 tablespoons whole wheat or white flour
   ¼ teaspoon vanilla extract
   1 tablespoon butter or margarine

Mix all ingredients except butter or margarine in a blender until smooth.

Melt butter or margarine in a skillet. Pour in mixture to make 3 inch diameter pancakes. Cook over medium heat. Flip when bottom browns.

Serve with applesauce, stewed dried fruit, or chopped fresh fruit.

Serves 2.

See also: Blender drinks in Chapter Nine.

Notes

1. Judith S. Stern, Sc.D., "Meals and Migraine," Vogue, March, 1984.
2. Kirschmann, John D., *Nutrition Almanac,* McGraw-Hill, 1979.
3. National Migraine Foundation.

Chapter Eight

Fatigue

Fatigue is one of those nebulous symptoms which could indicate anything from a simple lack of sleep to serious disease. Your fatigue may be related to your diet in terms of nutrition or when you eat certain types of food. If you find yourself unaccountably tired at about the same time every day, especially after lunch, your fatigue is likely to be related to what you eat.

My father, who has relished the sweetness of surrendering to his metabolism, has been known to say after a big meal, "And now, it is time to take a small schluffy." This is a fine philosophy on a Sunday when you have the afternoon free for napping, but during the week you'll probably want your daytime meals less sedating.

What you eat, as well as how much, can greatly affect how alert you feel. Your blood sugar level influences chemicals in the brain which stimulate sleep and wakefulness. While your blood sugar level rises after eating anything, foods high in carbohydrates cause blood sugar to rise more rapidly. In addition, the more food you eat, the greater the rise in blood sugar. The higher your blood sugar level rises, the more insulin is secreted into your bloodstream. Insulin drives the amino acid, tryptophan, into the brain, which triggers the manufacture of serotonin, a neurotransmitter which causes sleepiness and lowered ability to concentrate.[1,2]

Foods which cause a rapid rise in blood sugar are high in simple carbohydrates: cakes and candy, large amounts of fruits and fruit juices, white bread, jam, pasta, and potatoes. High protein foods—poultry, fish, meat, dairy products, eggs, beans—and complex carbohydrates (whole grains) cause a more gradual rise in blood sugar level and stimulate the adrenalin pathway in your brain which keeps you awake and active.[3]

To avoid feeling tired after a meal, eat complex carbohydrates (whole grains) and/or vegetables with some kind of protein: beans, lean meats, low-fat dairy products. A breakfast of toast and jam or a doughnut may leave you feeling lethargic. Good breakfasts include whole grain toast with peanut butter and milk, hot cereal with milk and nuts, yogurt and granola. For lunch, a chef salad, tuna sandwich on whole wheat bread, vegetable soup or yogurt are all good choices.

Lack of Iron

You can feel tired from a lack of iron without suffering from anemia. Iron deficiencies are common, especially in women, and can make the body more vulnerable to viral infection, and less able to stay warm when it's cold out.

Absorption of iron in the body depends on several factors. Iron is absorbed more efficiently from lean red meats, poultry, and fish than from non-meat sources of iron: beans, grains, leafy vegetables and dried fruit. However, eating meat along with these non-meat foods enhances the iron absorption.[5]

Iron absorption is *inhibited* by chemicals (tannins and polyphenols) in tea and coffee (both regular and decaffeinated), egg yolks, too much fiber, soy protein, calcium supplements and antacids. The oxalic acid in spinach and rhubarb, and the phytate in eggplant, beet greens and lentils also inhibit iron absorption,[5] as do the food additives EDTA and phosphates which are added to soft drinks, baked goods and other foods.

You don't need to give up all these foods, just try to eat them separately from meals which contain major iron sources. Most researchers believe that fiber's inhibiting affect is too small to justify cutting it from the diet. While soy protein can inhibit iron absorption up to 80 percent, it is only a problem if used as a meat substitute as opposed to an addition to a meal containing meat.[6] Vegetarians may need to take an iron supplement. You can reduce the effect of coffee and tea on iron absorption by drinking them an hour *before* a meal rather than during or within an hour after a meal.[7]

Eating foods rich in vitamin C along with iron *enhances* iron absorption. The nutrients riboflavin and copper also aid in iron absorption. Cooking foods in an

Chronic fatigue may be a sign that
your diet is lacking in essential nutrients.

iron skillet will increase their iron content; in some cases, food cooked in an iron pan contains three or four times the iron it would have if cooked in a glass or aluminum pan.

Inhibitors of Iron Absorption

tea and coffee (regular and decaffeinated)
egg yolks
excess fiber
soy foods
spinach, rhubarb
eggplant, beet greens, lentils
calcium tablets
food additives EDTA and phosphates

Aids to Iron Absorption

vitamin C
eating meat along with grains and vegetables (only a small amount of meat is necessary)
cooking in iron pans
riboflavin (found in organ meats, cheese, almonds)
copper (found in nuts, beans, seafood)

Insomnia

According to the same theory that proposes what kinds of lunches will keep you alert, a high-carbohydrate snack before bed may have a relaxing effect. A late night snack such as dried fruit, juice or a cookie can cause your brain to produce the neurotransmitter serotonin, which is responsible for feelings of sleepiness and tranquility.[8]

The first set of recipes are examples of high-protein, iron rich dishes which may help fight fatigue. The Midnight Snacks are samples of high-carbohydrate foods which can stimulate your brain to release substances that aid in relaxation.

Seasoned Wheat Germ Liver

This dish is truly a member of the nutritionally elite. Loaded with protein, zinc, and vitamin A, liver is also one of the best sources of iron. The vitamin C in the green peppers aids in absorption of the iron.

1½ pounds calves liver, cut in ½ inch thick strips
⅔ cup wheat germ
½ teaspoon salt
1 teaspoon thyme
black pepper to taste
4 teaspoons fresh lemon juice
4 teaspoons sesame oil
1 green pepper, chopped
¼ cup vegetable or sesame oil for sautéing

Combine wheat germ, salt, thyme and pepper on a plate and mix well.
Mix lemon juice and sesame oil and brush on liver.
Coat liver pieces well with wheat germ mixture; let stand for about 10 minutes.
Heat the oil in a skillet over low-medium heat, add the green pepper and cook for 3 minutes, then add the liver and sauté for an additional 3 to 5 minutes.
Serves 4.

Norman's Yellow Mung Bean Soup

This flavorful soup is a hit with bean-eating beginners and veterans alike. Mung beans contain iron, riboflavin, copper, and make a complete protein when served with a grain.

> 8 cups water
> 1 large onion cut into rings
> 3-4 cloves garlic, sliced thin or pressed
> 1 tablespoon allspice
> ½ teaspoon freshly grated ginger
> 2 teaspoons thyme
> 1 teaspoon cumin seed (try to use this spice, but if you don't have it, use ½ teaspoon cumin powder)
> 1 to 2 teaspoons salt
> ½ teaspoon white pepper
> 2½ to 3½ dried split mung beans
> 3 carrots, sliced
> 1 tomato, diced into small pieces

Add water and onions to a big pot and bring to a boil. Add spices, mung beans, carrots and tomato.
Lower heat and cover with lid, leaving a little space open between lid and pot.
Stir occasionally. Mung beans will split and start forming broth after 15 minutes.
Cook for 1½ hours to 2 hours.
May be served immediately, but it's even more delicious if you store it in the fridge over night, letting the flavors steep and the soup thicken.
Makes about 2 quarts.

Almond-Walnut Spread

Almonds and walnuts are good sources of iron, copper, and riboflavin. Spread on toast or crackers and accompany with a glass of milk for an empowering, high protein breakfast.

> ¼ cup almonds and walnuts, mixed
> 1 tablespoon vegetable oil
> 2 teaspoon lemon juice
> pinch of salt

Combine ingredients in a blender. You will probably have to stop the blender after a few seconds and stir the mixture with a long handled spoon or a chopstick, and then start again.
Spread on bread or whole grain crackers, or stir a spoonful into hot cereal.
Makes ¼ cup.

Midnight Snacks

You can eat any high-carbohydrate food, such as crackers or leftover rice or potatoes. Just remember that it's a *snack*—going to bed with a full stomach may keep you awake, give you indigestion, and make you feel generally lousy in the morning.

Other Suggestions

- Slice a banana in half, drizzle with honey and sprinkle with wheat germ. Broil for 5 minutes.
- Stew any dried fruit with a little water for 5 minutes in a saucepan, spread on toast.
- Pop popcorn in an air popper. (Oil or butter can make digestion difficult.)
- Make Oatmeal-Banana-Nut cookies in PMS chapter.

Notes

1. Mirkin, Dr. Gabe, "Lunches to keep you alert," May 7, 1985.

2. Morgan, Dr. Brian L.G. Morgan, "The Amazing Power of Food," Family Circle, August 2, 1983.
3. Ehret, Dr. Charles F., *Overcoming Jet Lag,* Berkley Books, New York, 1983.
4. Aronson, Virginia, R.D., M.S., "Ironing Out Your Diet," *Runner's World,* October 1985.
5. Malesky, Gale, "What You Don't Know About Iron Can't Help You," *Prevention,* March, 1984.
6. Ibid.
7. Aronson, Op. Cit.
8. Morgan, Brian, M.D., "The Amazing Power of Food," *Family Circle,* August 2, 1983.

Chapter Nine

The Ailing Athlete

Injuries

Maintaining a well-balanced diet is essential after an injury when your body is trying to repair and rebuild itself. Certain nutrients have been isolated as especially important to promote internal healing:

zinc: Experiments have shown that wounds in animals with low levels of zinc healed slowly, and that zinc supplementation restored normal healing.[1] Zinc sources: pumpkin seeds, sunflower seeds, liver, cheese, wheat germ, whole-grains, brewer's yeast.

vitamin A: Recent experiments indicate that vitamin A accelerates the healing of skin incisions and increases the number of white blood cells at the injured area.[2] While active vitamin A is found only in animal foods, our bodies also synthesize vitamin A from beta-carotene (in vegetables and fruits) when needed. Sources of vitamin A: milk, butter, liver, carrots, broccoli, leafy greens, red peppers, peaches, eggs, sweet potatoes, prunes.

vitamin C: Extravagant claims aside, vitamin C is essential to proper healing of wounds; one of its most crucial roles is in the formation and maintenance of

Pumpkin seeds are rich in zinc, a nutrient essential to the proper healing
of injuries.

collagen, the protein of connective and scar tissue. Vitamin C thins synovial fluid, the lubricating fluid that nourishes cartilage, allowing it to move more freely in the joints.[3] Synovial fluid is vital to the healing of torn cartilage, since cartilage does not receive nourishment from the blood. Vitamin C sources: citrus fruits, green peppers, broccoli, brussels sprouts, kale, parsley, cauliflower, potatoes, tomatoes, honeydew melons, cantaloupe.

magnesium: This mineral is essential to wound healing because it activates many enzymes involved in energy production and protein synthesis.[4] Magnesium sources: fresh green vegetables, raw wheat germ, soybeans, figs, corn, apples, seeds and nuts, especially almonds.

Cramping and Fatigue

Cramping and fatigue may indicate a mineral imbalance. While deficiencies in the minerals potassium, sodium, and magnesium are relatively rare, iron deficiency is common among athletes who train hard. You can be iron deficient without being anemic, causing you to tire earlier when you exercise because your body cannot clear lactic acid properly.[5] You can prevent or correct iron deficiency by eating an iron-rich diet. See your doctor before taking an iron supplement. Chapter Eight discusses how to remedy an iron deficiency in more detail.

Eating Before Exercise

If you skip breakfast the day of an athletic event, your blood sugar level is likely to drop and you could find yourself tired during competition.[6] Most sports experts recommend eating a small meal of 500 to 1,000 calories about three to four hours before competition or work-out so that digestion does not interfere with performance.[7] A low-fat, low-protein, high carbohydrate meal is easily digested: fat delays digestion and too much protein can cause dehydration and may strain the kidneys.[8]

Eating a large amount of sugar before competition will wear you out early. Insulin released in response to the sugar will end up making less glucose available for fuel.[9]

A liquid meal is easy to digest and may be taken up to two hours prior to competition.

Adequate fluid intake cannot be overemphasized. Athletes lose a lot of water through perspiration and increased respiration. Dehydration can cause fatigue, muscle cramps, and loss of consciousness. Athletes should drink cold water before an event, during events lasting more than thirty minutes, and after every event.[10] Sports drinks, soft drinks, and juices are not the best fluid replacers because they contain a high amount of sugar which delays absorption.

Tiredness after competition is usually caused by a lack of stored muscle sugar.[11] You can recover faster from strenuous exercise by eating extra carbohydrates.[12] An athlete's daily diet should also emphasize carbohydrates to ensure storage of sugar in the muscles and liver for energy.

Recipes

Sesame Chicken Stir-Fry

Chicken is low in fat, easily digested, and a fine source of protein and iron. Vitamin A in the broccoli and carrots, vitamin C in the peas and broccoli, and zinc in the mushrooms—all nutrients important for healing.

1 pound boneless, skinless chicken breasts
1 tablespoon sesame seeds
2 tablespoons soy sauce
⅛ to ¼ teaspoon black pepper
3 teaspoons vegetable oil
1 cup carrots, sliced thin
1 cup broccoli, in flowerets or small trees
10 to 12 snow pea pods
½ cup mushrooms
small can water chestnuts
½ cup chicken broth
1½ cups scallions, sliced
1 tablespoon arrowroot or cornstarch, mixed with ½ cup cold water

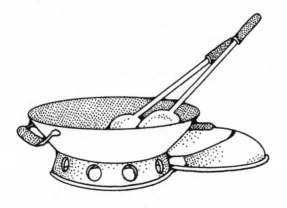

Cut chicken into thin strips, slicing against grain.
Mix soy sauce, 2 teaspoons oil, pepper, and sesame seeds in a small bowl.
Add chicken and let stand for at least 5 minutes.
Heat a nonstick skillet over moderately high heat.
Cook chicken for 3 to 5 minutes, stirring constantly.
Remove chicken when it is just cooked through; set aside.
Add remaining teaspoon of oil to pan. Add carrots and broccoli; stir for 1 minute.
Add broth, cover, and simmer for 2 to 3 minutes. Add the remaining vegetables and cook another minute.
Stir in chicken, scallions and arrowroot or cornstarch mixture; stir until boiling. Cover and simmer another 2 minutes.
Serves 4.

Pumpkin Seeds

You can buy pumpkin seeds in the store, but they'll taste better if you roast them yourself. Pumpkin seeds are an excellent source of zinc.

    pumpkin
    tamari or soy sauce

Open pumpkin, remove seeds, wash away pulp, blot dry. Spread seeds out on a lightly oiled cookie sheet and bake in a 350 °F. oven for about 15 minutes.
Remove and place in a warm frying pan. Drizzle with tamari and stir to coat for another minute.

Wheat Germ Muffins With A Lot Extra

These muffins provide zinc, magnesium and a good dose of complex carbohydrates. Good for breakfast and snacks, and as a high-carbohydrate pick-me-up after a workout.

1½ cups whole wheat flour
1 cup wheat germ
½ teaspoon salt
1 tablespoon baking powder
6 tablespoon nonfat dry milk powder or
    soy milk powder
1 cup water
1 egg, lightly beaten
3 tablespoons oil
2 tablespoons honey or molasses
¼ to ½ cup raisins
¼ cup sunflower seeds
¼ cup chopped almonds

Preheat oven to 400 °F.
Combine dry ingredients in one bowl, liquid in another. Slowly add liquid ingredients to dry, stirring only enough to moisten. Don't worry about lumps.
Spoon into oiled muffin tin.
Bake for 20 to 25 minutes.
Makes 12 muffins.

Liquid Meals

Good the day of a competition, or when you'll be exercising within an hour or two of a meal.

Fruity Milk Shake

½ cup fruit: banana, strawberries, peaches, etc.
½ cup apple juice
½ cup orange juice
¼ cup nonfat dry milk powder or
    soy milk powder
3 ice cubes
Blend ingredients in blender.
Makes a cup and a half of fruity froth.

Protein Shake

½ cup yogurt
½ cup low-fat milk
½ banana
½ cup apple juice
1 tablespoon soy powder (optional)
1 teaspoon vanilla

Blend in blender.
Makes almost 2 cups.

Morning Blaster

This should power you through lunch.

½ cup cranberry juice
½ cup apple juice
2 tablespoons wheat germ
2 tablespoons bran
1 egg (optional)
1 tablespoon safflower oil (optional)
1 tablespoon molasses (optional)
1 tablespoon soy powder (optional)
1 tablespoon brewer's yeast (don't add it unless you can tolerate (or even enjoy) its unique flavor)

Blend well, drink, and fly out the door.
Makes 2 to 3 cups.

Notes

1. Hunt, Thomas K. and J. Englebert Dunphy, Fundamentals of Wound Management, Appleton-Century-Crofts, N.Y., 1979.
2. Ibid.
3. Kirschmann, John D., ed., *Nutrition Almanac,* McGraw-Hill, 1979.
4. Hunt, Op. Cit.
5. Dr. Gabe Mirkin, M.D., "Iron Deficiency without Anemia," May 7, 1985.
6. Dr. Gabe Mirkin, M.D., "Nutrition changes for athletes," April 16, 1985.

7. Richard B. Birrer, Ed., *Sports Medicine for the Primary Care Physician*, Appleton-Century Crofts, Newark, Connecticut, 1984.
8. Ibid.
9. Foster, et al., "Effects of pre-exercise feedings on endurance performance," *Med. Sci. Sports*, 11:1, 1979.
10. Mirkin, Op. cit.
11. Ibid.
12. Shangold, Mona, M.D., and Mirkin, Gabe, M.D., *The Complete Sports Medicine Book for Women*, Simon & Schuster, New York, 1985.

PART 4
Women's Section

Chapter Ten

PMS
Premenstrual Syndrome

PMS—now there's a name for it, but women have long known that a variety of uncomfortable symptoms can accompany hormonal changes in the body. Recent research has found that the particular "syndrome" that a woman with PMS experiences usually falls into one of four or five groups of symptoms.

According to Dr. Guy Abraham, who has researched extensively on PMS, different symptoms indicate different chemical imbalances in the body. He classifies PMS into four subgroups: women with Type A PMS, the most common syndrome, suffer primarily from anxiety, irritability and mood swings. Those with Type H have symptoms of abdominal bloating, breast tenderness and weight gain. Type C PMS is characterized by increased appetite, sugar craving, fatigue and headaches. Women whose major PMS symptom is depression (Type D) are less common and often more difficult to treat.[1]

While some doctors do not believe a nutritional approach to PMS is valid, according to Abraham and several other physicians specializing in treatment of premenstrual difficulties, most women with PMS respond quite favorably to nutritional treatment. Treatment may also involve a progesterone prescription. In many cases, however, PMS sufferers have nutritional imbalances which aggravate their conditions and can be corrected with a proper diet.

What's Happening?

Type A: Anxiety, irritability, nervous tension

The menstrual cycle involves a delicate balance of hormones which is very sensitive to conditions such as emotional stress and nutritional deficiencies. An improper balance of the hormones estrogen and progesterone can influence a woman's moods. Excess estrogen tends to stimulate anxiety, while progesterone has a depressive effect.

Elevated estrogen levels have been found in women with Type A PMS. Dr. Abraham's research suggests that vitamin B complex and magnesium deficiencies, which interfere with the liver's metabolism of estrogen, result in this imbalance of estrogen and progesterone, which then cause anxiety and irritability.[2]

In addition, Dr. Abraham found that women with Type A PMS consumed five times more dairy products and three times more refined sugar than other women. Dairy products, excess calcium and refined sugar can all contribute to magnesium deficiency.[3] To make matters worse, animal fats contain a substance which interferes with the production of progesterone, making a diet high in dairy products, meat and sweetened foods a disaster for PMS sufferers.

Women with Type A PMS should build their diets around foods rich in B vitamins and magnesium—whole grains, beans, nuts and vegetables—while reducing their consumption of meat, sugar and dairy products.

Type C: Fatigue, headache, craving for sweets

Several factors can cause the sugar craving, headaches and fatigue that many women experience before their menstrual cycle. A woman's body uses insulin, which removes glucose from the bloodstream, more readily a week before her period.[4] Her blood sugar level is therefore likely to drop, making less sugar available for the brain and triggering symptoms of weakness, irritability, sugar craving and headache.

Nutrients important to processes which moderate blood sugar level include magnesium, zinc, vitamin C, vitamin B_6 and cis-linoleic acid (an essential fatty acid found in vegetable oils). Salt and animal fats can aggravate this type of PMS as well.[5]

Type H: Bloating, breast tenderness, weight gain

The retention of fluid and sodium in the tissues is responsible for Type H PMS symptoms. Dr. Abraham's research found that stress, sugar consumption and deficiencies in magnesium and vitamin B_6 can all lead to sodium and water retention. Eating salty foods will aggravate this condition.[6]

Type D: Depression

This type of PMS was noted in only five percent of the women Abraham studied. Women with Type D PMS have low levels of estrogen. Again, Abraham found that B vitamin and magnesium deficiencies worsened this condition.[7]

The PMS Diet

Any inconvenience posed by changing your eating

habits should be outweighed by the benefits of this diet. Many women who have adjusted their diets to these guidelines have had their PMS symptoms disappear.

AVOID:	**BECAUSE:**
1. Caffeine	• increases need for B vitamins; important for glucose metabolism, deactivation of estrogen by liver. • can worsen breast swelling, tenderness, headaches, irritability.
2. Salt	• increases fluid retention • breast tenderness • too much salt causes potassium deficiency, which can cause muscle cramping. Potassium regulates body's water balance.
3. Refined Sugar	• depletes B vitamins and magnesium • triggers vicious cycle of insulin production which lowers blood sugar level, causing sugar craving. • contributes to fluid retention
4. Alcohol	• depletes B vitamins • interferes with carbohydrate metabolism

AVOID:	BECAUSE:

5. High fat meats (beef, pork, lamb)
- animal fat affects the liver's ability to metabolize hormones.

6. Excess dairy products
- Excess calcium depletes magnesium in body. Magnesium is essential for the absorption of calcium and other nutrients, helps ease cramps, and helps reduce nervousness and mood swings.

EMPHASIZE:

1. Whole Grains
- good sources of fiber, B vitamins, vitamin E, minerals
- helps stabilize blood sugar level

2. Legumes
- complete protein with grains
- lower in fat than meat

3. Seeds and Nuts
- magnesium, protein, B complex vitamins, unsaturated fat

4. Vegetables and Fruits
- good sources of vitamins and minerals, especially A, C and potassium. Natural fiber improves glucose tolerance.

Note: Some women may be puzzled by the advice to cut their consumption of dairy products, especially if

Animal fat, alcohol, caffeine, refined
sugar & salt can spell disaster for
women with **PMS**.

they have been conscientiously trying to increase their calcium intake to prevent the bone disease osteoporosis, or because they've heard that calcium eases menstrual cramps. Calcium *is* a vital nutrient, and many of us don't get enough of it. The key to remember is that magnesium aids in the proper absorption of calcium, while calcium interferes with the absorption of magnesium. In order to prevent a magnesium deficiency, many researchers recommend a diet with a magnesium/calcium ratio of 2:1. *If you consume an adequate amount of magnesium, your body will be able to absorb more calcium from the calcium-containing foods you do eat.*

Recipes

High Protein dishes low in or without animal fats:

Joel's Chicken Limón

Chicken is low in fat, high in protein, and contains B vitamins and iron.

    4 boneless, skinless chicken breasts
    2 scallions, sliced in ½ inch rounds
    ¼ pound fresh sliced mushrooms
    ¼ cup white wine
    1 tablespoon flour
    2 tablespoons butter
    3 lemons

Pound the chicken breasts with a mallet until thin.
Sauté the chicken, mushrooms, and scallions in butter.
Juice two of the lemons and add to the simmering chicken.
Thinly slice the third lemon and sauté in the same pan.
Pour wine and flour into a small jar, and cover. Shake jar until the flour mixes completely with the wine.
Pour the mixture into the pan and stir.
Simmer until the sauce thickens and serve with brown rice.
Serves 3 to 4.

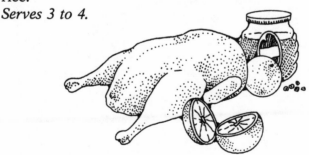

Delectable Almond Chicken

Almonds are an especially good source of magnesium.

> 4 chicken breasts, skinless and boneless, sliced into strips
> 1 large onion, minced
> 1 tablespoon margarine
> ½ teaspoon cumin
> ½ teaspoon thyme
> ¼ teaspoon cayenne
> 1 cup raw almonds, ground in blender or food processor
> 2 tablespoons fresh parsley, chopped
> 1 teaspoon tamari
> 1 clove garlic, pressed
> 2 tablespoons mayonnaise
> water for thinning

Steam chicken until just cooked through, 10 to 15 minutes.

Sauté onions in margarine over low heat. Add cumin, thyme, and cayenne. Cook until onions are soft.

In a separate bowl, combine almonds, parsley, tamari, garlic and mayonnaise. Thin with water until it is the consistency of a thick sauce.

Add chicken to onions in pan, stir, and pour sauce over mixture.

Serves 3 to 4.

Tofu Sloppy Joes

Tofu is low in fat, high in magnesium and calcium. Whole grain buns provide B vitamins and make a complete protein with tofu.

1 tablespoon vegetable oil
½ onion, chopped
½ green pepper, chopped
½ cup mushrooms, chopped
8 ounces tofu
2 teaspoons parsley
½ teaspoon each oregano and sweet basil
½ clove minced or pressed garlic
8 ounces tomato sauce
2 tablespoons tamari or soy sauce

Sauté onions and mushrooms in oil.
Add crumbled tofu to pan. Add spices, mix.
Add tomato sauce and tamari. Let simmer for 15 minutes.
Serve on whole grain buns with lettuce and tomato.
Serves 3 to 4.

Miso Vegetable Soup

Miso, fermented soybean paste, is a complete protein and good for digestion. Since miso tends to contain a moderate to high amount of sodium, look for low-sodium miso in Oriental or health food stores. This soup is ideal for women with PMS: magnesium in the rice, millet and potatoes; vitamin B_6 in the rice, greens, broccoli and other vegetables.

> 2 quarts water
> 1 large onion, chopped
> 2 cloves garlic, pressed or minced
> 1 large potato chopped
> ½ cup brown rice, bulgur or millet
> 2 cups broccoli, chopped
> 2 cups other vegetable, chopped: zucchini, cauliflower, green pepper, leeks
> 1 cup washed greens (kale, spinach, beet greens)
> 1 tablespoon miso
> 1 egg
> 2 teaspoons tamari or soy sauce
> pinch cayenne pepper

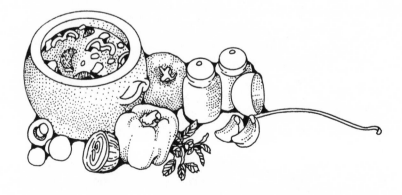

In a large pot, boil water while you chop vegetables.

Add onion, garlic, potato and grain to boiling water, turn heat to medium and simmer for about 8 minutes.

Add the harder vegetables first (broccoli, cauliflower) and let cook for 5 minutes.

Add the rest of the vegetables, cook for 5 minutes longer. Add the greens, stir, and remove from heat.

In a small bowl, mix the miso, egg, tamari, and cayenne pepper briskly with a fork or whisk.

Add to soup, stir and let stand a moment before serving.

Variations: To boost the protein content, add leftover chopped chicken, or cubes of tofu or tempeh (steam tempeh first for 10 minutes) before adding vegetables.

Serves 8.

Parsley Pepper Sauce for rice or noodles

This sauce is low in fat, but rich in flavor and nutrients. Parsley and pepper are high in vitamin C; tofu or chick peas with rice or noodles provides complete protein.

> ⅔ cup green pepper, chopped
> ⅓ cup fresh parsley, chopped
> 1 tablespoon lemon juice
> 1 tablespoon tahini
> 1 clove garlic, pressed
> 1 teaspoon basil
> ½ cup water
> 4 ounces tofu, cut in cubes or
>   4 ounces canned chick peas

Blend all ingredients except tofu in a blender.
Pour into a saucepan, add tofu or chick peas and heat slowly to boiling.
Turn down heat and simmer for 10 to 15 minutes.
Serve over brown rice, spinach noodles or whole grain pasta.
Serves 2.

Orange Miso Dressing

Here's a salad dressing for both fruit and vegetable salads. Simple to make, but low in fat, high in protein and vitamin C.

2 teaspoons miso
½ cup orange juice, preferably fresh squeezed
2 tablespoons tahini

Blend in blender. Serve over salad. Especially good over . . .

Tropical Salad

Fresh parsley is essential for this refreshing salad.

1 small head of red leaf lettuce
½ avocado, cut in small chunks
½ green pepper, chopped
¼ cup chopped fresh parsley
⅛ cup slivered almonds
¼ cup pineapple in small chunks, fresh or packed
in its own juice

Combine all ingredients in a bowl. Toss to mix well.
Serves 3 to 4.

Replacements for Dairy Products

To make any of the following "milks," blend the indicated ingredients in a blender. After you've made a couple of mixtures you will begin to improvise with ingredients and won't need recipes. You can add extra fruit—blueberries, peaches, apples—to any recipe, or flavor extracts. Bananas are ideal for these concoctions because they add richness and bulk without adding fat.

Nut Milk

> ½ cup almonds or cashews
> 1 teaspoon vanilla
> ½ cup apple juice
> ½ cup water
> 2 ice cubes

Makes 1 cup.

Sesame Milk

> ½ cup apple juice
> ½ cup water
> 2-3 ice cubes
> 3 tablespoons tahini
> ½ banana

Soy Milk

> 1 tablespoon soy powder
> ½ cup apple or grape juice
> ½ cup water
> 2 ice cubes
> ½ banana
> ½ peach, fresh or packed in its own juice
> ½ teaspoon cinnamon

Pina Colada Milk

1 teaspoon unsweetened shredded coconut
½ cup water
½ cup pineapple juice
4-5 pineapple chunks
½ banana
3 ice cubes
1 tablespoon soy powder

Serve this over fruit or as a dessert beverage.

Treats

While you wean yourself from sweets, experiment with recipes for treats that include healthy ingredients, and derive sweetness from fresh and dried fruits and juices. Remember that even healthy goodies can upset your blood sugar level, so try to eat these with a meal, and limit yourself to about three a day.

Figgies

Figs are a good source of magnesium.

> 1 cup dried figs
> 2 tablespoons lemon juice
> ½ cup walnuts
> ½ cup sunflower seeds
> unsweetened coconut flakes

Soak figs in boiling water and lemon juice brought to a simmer for 10 minutes. Drain.
Chop the figs, walnuts and sunflower seeds in a blender. Shape the mixture in little balls and roll in coconut.
Makes 15 to 20 balls.

Oatmeal-Banana-Nut Cookies

Delicious without any added sugar or honey.

>1 cup oats
>1 cup whole wheat flour
>⅓ cup oil
>⅓ cup chopped nuts
>½ cup raisins (or chopped dates or figs)
>1 mashed banana
>½ cup apple juice

Mix oats and flour. Stir in oil.
Add mashed banana and apple juice, then nuts and raisins.
Drop by spoonfuls onto oiled cookie sheet.
Bake at 350°F. for 30 minutes.
Makes about 2 dozen.

Foods with a good magnesium/calcium ratio[8]:

millet	wheat
brown rice	peanuts
corn	potato
oats	almonds

Good Sources of Vitamin B_6[9]:

salmon	navy beans
rye flour	beet greens
chicken	lima beans
brown rice	buckwheat flour
tuna	green peas
broccoli	sunflower seeds
soybeans	pinto beans
asparagus	sweet potatoes
rice bran	shrimp
wheat germ	whole wheat flour
kale	leeks
brussels sprouts	black-eyed peas
lentils	cauliflower
torula yeast	brewer's yeast

Notes

1. Abraham, Guy E., M.D., "Nutrition and the Premenstrual Tension Syndromes," *Journal of Applied Nutrition,* 36:2, 1984.
2. Ibid.
3. Ibid.
4. DePirro, Fusco, Bertoli, et al, "Insulin receptors during the menstrual cycle in normal women," *Journal of Clinical Endocrinology Metabolism,* 47:1387, 1978.

5. Abraham, Guy E., M.D., "Nutritional Factors in the Etiology of the Premenstrual Tension Syndromes," *Journal of Reproductive Medicine,* 28:7, July 1983.
6. Ibid.
7. Ibid.
8. Lark, Susan, M.D., *The Premenstrual Syndrome Self-Help Book,* Forman, Los Angeles, 1984.
9. Ibid.

Chapter Eleven

Pregnancy

Some of the minor health problems experienced by pregnant women can be improved with diet. Pregnancy greatly increases a woman's nutritional needs, and a good diet promotes better health for the mother and infant, an easier delivery and a greater chance to nurse successfully. The pregnant woman's diet should feature nutrient dense foods—foods with a high concentration of nutrients per serving.

Nutrient Dense Foods

Asparagus
Beans
Broccoli
Cantaloupe
Citrus Fruits
Dark, leafy greens
Fish
Nuts and Seeds
Poultry
Sprouts
Wheat Germ
Yogurt

Bananas
Brewer's Yeast
Cabbage
Carrots
Cheese
Eggs
Lean Meat
Peppers
Soy products
Sweet Potatoes
Whole Grains

Irritability, Fatigue

Levels of iron and folate (or folic acid) often drop during pregnancy.[1,2] Folate is a B vitamin essential for a normal pregnancy, and you can develop a folate deficiency if you do not get enough iron, or if your diet features mainly carbohydrates, which contain only small amounts of folate and iron.[3] Irritability, forgetfulness, and mental sluggishness can indicate a folate deficiency. Lack of energy, headaches, shortness of breath, and pale skin are symptoms of iron deficiency anemia. See the chapter on fatigue for more details about iron.

Good sources of iron: meats, dried beans and peas, green leafy vegetables, dried fruit (prunes and raisins).
Good sources of folate: leafy green vegetables, fruits, nuts, dried beans and peas.

Hypoglycemia

Hypoglycemia—abnormally low blood sugar—has become a garbage can explanation for vague symptoms such as depression and fatigue. Most doctors believe that the actual condition, which can be verified by a glucose tolerance test, is actually fairly rare. While the cause and mechanisms of hypoglycemia are not fully known, the general assumption is that in *some genetically predisposed people,* diet and/or stress can trigger hypoglycemic symptoms—shakiness before meals, depression, compulsive hunger for sweet foods, fatigue, and muscle weakness.

The stress of pregnancy and childbirth may result in hypoglycemia in susceptible women.[5] Diets high in sugar and other refined carbohydrates, and stimulants such as caffeine and nicotine, can result in hypoglycemia in some individuals.[6]

Controlling Hypoglycemia

To stabilize blood sugar level, eat breakfast and regular meals throughout the day. Emphasize protein and limit starches. When you do eat carbohydrates, choose foods prepared with whole grains (whole wheat bread, oatmeal, brown rice) rather than refined ones (white bread, white rice, Cream of Wheat). Brown rice and corn tend to cause less rapid changes in blood sugar level than do potatoes or wheat.[7]

High fiber foods are absorbed more slowly in the digestive tract. Dietary gums, pectins and mucilages are soluble fibers which can help control hypoglycemia. Beans, fruits, and oat bran are good sources of soluble fiber.[8] One study showed that drinking apple juice raised the insulin level in the blood twice as high as eating a whole apple, indicating that fiber improves glucose tolerance.[9]

Hemorrhoids

Most pregnant women who get hemorrhoids actually had them before they became pregnant; the pressure changes of pregnancy make them aware of their hemorrhoids for the first time.[10] Hemorrhoids are often associated with constipation and usually benefit from an increase in bulk (fiber) in the diet, as suggested in Chapter Five.

Morning Sickness

Eating dry crackers or toast before breakfast may help ease morning sickness. See the recipe in this chapter for delicious, whole-grain crackers. Otherwise, follow the general recommendations for avoiding indigestion: eat small meals, about two hours apart; avoid caffeine, spicy foods, excess butter and fat. Drink liquids in between meals rather than with meals.

The recipes in this chapter feature foods rich in iron, folate, protein, fiber and complex carbohydrates.

Brussels Sprouts in Ginger Garlic Sauce

Brussels sprouts are high in vitamin C, potassium, iron and folic acid. This sauce is also excellent over other vegetables—broccoli, kale—and rice or noodles. Serve with lean beef or chicken to increase iron absorption.

10 to 15 brussels sprouts
½ cup oil
2 tablespoons sesame oil
4 cloves garlic, pressed
2 tablespoons freshly grated ginger
2 tablespoons arrowroot or cornstarch
1½ cups water
⅓ cup soy sauce
2 tablespoons wine vinegar
1 tablespoon honey

Steam brussels sprouts for 10 to 15 minutes until tender. To prepare the sauce: Sauté garlic in the oils until translucent. Add grated ginger and let cook for about 5 minutes.
Dissolve the arrowroot in the water, stir in the soy sauce, vinegar, and honey, and add to saucepan.
Bring sauce to a boil, stirring constantly. Lower heat and let simmer until sauce has thickened (about 5 minutes).
Pour sauce over brussels sprouts and serve.
Serves 2 to 3.

Orange Bulgur Salad

Both oranges and bulgur are rich in folic acid and fiber.

1 cup bulgur
2 cups water
2 tablespoons orange juice concentrate
½ tablespoon lemon juice
½ tablespoon honey
dash salt
¼ teaspoon dry mustard
¼ cup oil
1 orange, peeled and sectioned

Prepare bulgur by adding grain to boiling water, covering, and letting simmer for 15 to 20 minutes. When grain is tender, refrigerate until cold.
For dressing: combine orange juice, lemon juice, honey, salt and mustard in a blender and blend until smooth.
Pour over cold bulgur and stir well.
Mix in orange sections.
Garnish with fresh parsley sprigs.
Serves 4.

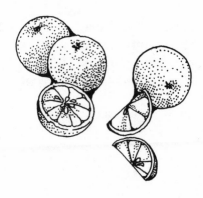

Good Cracker

Crackers are usually considered innocuous food, vehicles to carry cheese and dips to the mouth. These crackers, with a hint of orange flavor, are truly special and simple to make. As opposed to white flour crackers which provide little fiber or B vitamins, these wholesome crackers offer both in whole wheat flour, sesame seeds, and yogurt.

1 cup whole wheat flour
¼ teaspoon salt
2 tablespoons oil
1½ teaspoons honey
1 tablespoon orange
    juice concentrate
¼ cup yogurt
1 tablespoon sesame seeds

Preheat oven to 400°F.
Mix flour, salt and sesame seeds in a bowl.
Stir honey, oil, orange juice and yogurt together in a separate container and then add to flour, stirring to form a dough.
Roll out dough to about ⅛ inch thick on a lightly floured surface.
Transfer to a foil-covered baking sheet, score into squares, and bake for 10 minutes at 400°F. Peek in the oven after 8 minutes to be sure crackers aren't burning.
Makes 30 to 40 crackers, depending on size of squares.

Garbanzo Spread (Hummus)

When you have a yen for butter, jelly, or Cheez Whiz, spread this on your bread instead. Chick peas are low in saturated fat and an excellent source of complex carbohydrates, fiber, and folic acid. This spread makes a great sandwich with sliced banana and dates, or as a dip with fresh vegetables or sliced pita bread.

> 1 16 ounce can chick peas
> ¼ cup lemon juice
> 2 cloves garlic, pressed
> 2 teaspoons soy sauce
> 3 tablespoons tahini
> cayenne pepper to taste
> ¼ teaspoon ground cumin
> 2 tablespoons chopped fresh parsley

Purée chick peas in a blender. Add a little water if the mixture is too thick.
Add the rest of the ingredients and blend again. Refrigerate.
Makes 2 cups.

See also:
Best Bran Muffins in Chapter Five.
Wheat Germ Muffins in Chapter Nine.
All iron-rich recipes in Chapter Eight.

Notes

1. Childbirth Education Association, *Birth of a family*, Washington, D.C., 1980.
2. *Journal of Nutritional Science and Vitaminology*, vol. 23, 1977.

3. Pfeiffer, Carl C., *Intern. Journal of Environ. Studies*, 17:1, 43-46, May 1981.
4. Ibid.
5. Ibid.
6. Reiser, S., and Hallfrisch, J., "Blood Lipids and Their Distribution in Lipoproteins in Subjects Fed Three Levels of Sucrose," *Journal of Nutrition*, 111:1045, 1981.
7. Coulston, A., and Reaven, G., "Effect of Source of Dietary Carbohydrate on Plasma Glucose in Normal Subjects," *Amer. J. Clin. Nutrition*, 33:1279, 1980.
8. Liebman, Bonnie, "Facts on Fiber," *Nutrition Action*, Center for Science in the Public Interest.
9. Haber, E.B., et al: *Lancet*, 1977, (I) 679-682.
10. Holt, R.L., *Hemorrhoids: a Cure and Preventive*, William Morrow & Co., New York, 1980.

PART 5

Chapter Twelve

Hangovers

Alcohol causes the body to rid itself of fluids more quickly. Most of the ills associated with a hangover are due to dehydration. Headache, nausea, and bloodshot eyes can all be traced to dehydration.[1] The best way to remedy a hangover is to re-hydrate oneself by drinking an ample amount of (non-alcoholic) liquid. Coffee, despite its reputation as a "sobering" drink, can actually *prolong* a hangover because it acts as a diuretic, contributing to further dehydration. Non-citrus fruit juice (easier on the stomach than citrus) provides calories and nourishment along with fluid—especially important when even the mention of food leaves one feeling queasy.[2]

Nutrition

Alcohol can deplete the body of vitamin C and B vitamins. The aspirin you may take for a hangover will increase your need for vitamin C. Drinking an excessive amount of alcohol can also cause your body to excrete magnesium. A deficiency of magnesium can cause nausea, weakness, tremors and irritability.[3]

Oranges, grapefruits, and their juices are good sources of vitamin C, but may irritate a sensitive stomach. Cantaloupe is a soothing alternative. For a later meal, broccoli, brussels sprouts, green peppers, cauliflower and potatoes are excellent sources of vitamin C. Get the B's from lean beef, brewer's yeast, brown rice, chicken, kidney beans, sunflower seeds, wheat germ. Some of the best food sources of magnesium are soybeans, black-eyed peas, almonds, tofu, cashews, kidney beans, pecans, whole wheat, walnuts, banana, potato and oatmeal.

Two sample recipes follow which contain nutrients depleted by alcohol. Of course, you may not be able to stomach them until later in the day, or perhaps even the next day.

B-Rich Blender Drink

This drink is full of B vitamins, with additional magnesium in the banana, almonds, and sesame seeds.

1 tablespoon each of:
    almonds
    sunflower seeds
    sesame seeds
    wheat germ
    soy powder
    powdered milk
1 banana
¼ teaspoon cinnamon
½ cup water
½ cup apple or grape juice
3 to 4 ice cubes

Grind seeds and nuts until fine.
Combine with rest of ingredients in a blender; blend until smooth.
Makes 2 cups.

Potatoes Stuffed with Dressed Vegetables

This recipe uses vegetables rich in vitamin C, and dresses them with a hummus-like sauce full of B vitamins.

> 2 good sized potatoes
> ½ cup each, chopped:
> > broccoli
> > cauliflower
> > green pepper
>
> For Sauce:
> 1 cup cooked chick peas, drained
> 1 tablespoon oil
> ⅓ cup water
> 1 tablespoon tahini (sesame sauce)
> 1 tablespoon lemon juice
> 1 clove garlic
> 2 teaspoons soy sauce
> dash of cayenne pepper

Bake potatoes at 400°F. for 45 minutes to an hour until cooked through.

Steam vegetables for about 10 minutes; do not overcook.

To make sauce, combine last eight ingredients in a blender or food processor and process until smooth. Thin with more water if necessary.

Transfer sauce to a saucepan and heat gently over low heat. Do not boil. Add vegetables and stir.

Split potatoes and spoon in dressed vegetables.

Serves 2.

Notes

1. Freud, Clement, *Hangovers,* Sheldon Press, London, 1981.

2. Galton, Lawrence, *1,001 Health Tips*, Simon and Schuster, New York, 1984.
3. Linn, Dr. Robert, *You Can Drink and Stay Healthy*, Franklin Watts, New York, 1979.

Index

Flax seed, and constipation, 52
Fluid intake, and fever, 1, 10
    and exercise, 92
    and diarrhea, 44
Folate, and pregnancy, 124
Food allergies, viii
    and migraines, 70-71

G

Garlic, and colds, 1
    and indigestion, 30
    and constipation, 52
Gas, 32-35

H

Hangovers, 133-137
Headaches, 69-75
    and iron, 124
Heartburn, 35
Hemicellulose, and constipation, 51
Hemorrhoids, 125
Herpes, 17-27
Horseradish, and colds, 1
Hypoglycemia, 124

I

Indigestion, 29-41
Insomnia, 82
Iron, and fatigue, 79-81
    and pregnancy, 124
Irritable bowel syndrome, 43
Irritability, and folate, 124

K

Kudzo powder, and ulcers, 63

L

Lactose intolerance, 33-34, 43, 53
Low blood sugar, and headaches, 70
Lysine, and herpes, 18, 19, 21

M

Magnesium, and injuries, 91
    and PMS, 102, 103, 105
    and alcohol, 133
Migraines, 70-71
Milk, and ulcers, 62
Morning sickness, 125
Mustard, and colds, 1

N

Niacin, and indigestion, 32
Nutrition, basic, ix-x

O

Okra powder, and ulcers, 63
Olive Oil, 32
Oxalic acid, and iron absorption, 79

P

Papaya enzyme, 32
Parsley, and indigestion, 32
Pectin, and diarrhea, 44
Phytates, 40, 79
Pineapple, 32
Plantain bananas, and ulcers, 63
Potato, 32
Pregnancy, 123-131
Premenstrual syndrome, 101-121
Progesterone, and PMS, 101, 102
Psyllium seed, and constipation

S

Saurkraut, and constipation, 52
Serotonin, and fatigue, 77
    and insomnia
Slippery elm powder, and ulcers, 63
Smoking, and nutrition, ix
    and heartburn, 35
    and ulcers, 61
Sorbitol, and diarrhea, 43
Sour pickles, and constipation, 52
Sour rye bread, and constipation, 52

Sugar, and nutrition, x
and diarrhea, 10, 44
and B vitamin deficiency, 71
and athetic competition, 92
and PMS, 102-104
and hypoglycemia, 124
Synovial fluid, 91

T

Tabasco sauce, and colds, 1
Tannins, and constipation, 43, 49
and diarrhea, 47
and iron absorption, 79
Tempeh, 40
Tryptophan, and fatigue, 77

U

Ulcers, 61-67

V

Vitamin A, and ulcers, 62
and injuries, 89
Vitamin B, and indigestion, 32
and ulcers, 62
and headaches, 71
and PMS, 102-105
and alcohol, 133
Vitamin C, and alcohol
chewable, 30
high doses, 43
and injuries, 89
and iron absorption
and ulcers, 62
Vitamin E, and ulcers, 62

W

Wheat-gluten sensitivity, 43

X

xylitol, and diarrhea, 43

Y

Yogurt, and digestive bacteria, 33
and diarrhea, 44
and constipation, 52

Z

Zinc, and injuries, 89

Recipes

A

A-B-C-E loaf, 64
Almond chicken, 109
Almond-walnut spread, 85
Apple-raisin medley, 55

B

Banana freeze, 11
Barbecued beans, 23
Bean soup, 25
Blueberry spread, 47
Bran muffins, 59
B-Rich blender drink, 135
Brussels sprouts in ginger garlic sauce, 127
Bulgar breakfast cereal, 56
Bulgar with broccoli, 66

C

Carrot soup, 45
Chicken Limón,
Chicken soup, 4
Cottage cheese topping, 47
Crackers, 129

E

Egg drop soup, 14

F

Figgies, 118
Frozen apple yogurt, 13
Fruit gel, 12
Fruity milk shake, 97

144

G

Garbanzo spread, 130

L

Lemon squash, 15
Liquid breakfast, 54

M

Millet, 36
Miso vegetable soup, 111
Morning blaster, 98
Mung bean soup, 84

N

Noodle soup, 26
Nut milk, 116

O

Orange bulgur salad, 128
Orange-miso dressing, 114

P

Parsley dressing, 41
Parsley pepper sauce, 113
Pina colada milk, 117
Potatoes stuffed with dressed vegetables, 136
Protein shake, 97
Pumpkin seeds, 95

S

Seasoned wheat germ liver
Sesame chicken stir-fry
Sesame milk
Soy milk
Spaghetti sauce
Spiced apple sauce
Spiced miso broth
Spicy broccoli

T

Tofu sloppy joes
Tropical salad
Tsimmes

V
Vegetable miso soup

W
Wheat germ muffins